CHRISTMAS COOKIE SWAP!

CHRISTMAS COOKIE SWAP!

MORE THAN 100 TREATS TO
SHARE THIS HOLIDAY SEASON

Oxmoor
House®

Editor: Nicole Fisher
Project Editor: Melissa Brown
Designer: Allison Chi
Assistant Production Director: Sue Chodakiewicz
Senior Production Manager: Greg A. Amason
Copy Editors: Adrienne Davis, Jacqueline Giovanelli
Proofreaders: Norma Butterworth-McKittrick, Polly Linthicum
Indexer: Mary Ann Laurens

ISBN-13: 978-0-8487-4958-3
ISBN-10: 0-8487-4958-8
Library of Congress Control Number: 2016944944

First Edition 2016

Printed in the United States of America

10 9 8 7 6 5 4 3 2 1

Time Inc. Books products may be purchased for business or promotional use. For information on bulk purchases, please contact Christi Crowley in the Special Sales Department at (845) 895-9858.

We welcome your comments and suggestions about Time Inc. Books.
Please write to us at:
Time Inc. Books
Attention: Book Editors
P.O. Box 62310
Tampa, Florida 33662-2310

TABLE OF CONTENTS

MERRY CHRISTMAS!

Nothing compares to a homemade gift, especially if it comes from a warm oven. The smell of sugar, butter, and flour transforming into scrumptious cookies is the perfect reminder that it's the holidays. In this book you will find the ultimate cookie swap guide along with seasonal recipes and wrapping tips ensuring a special selection of sweet treats to savor with friends and family. Because the only thing better than sharing with the ones you love is enjoying a glass of cold milk and freshly-baked cookies with them, too.

CHRISTMAS COOKIE BASICS

Use a colorful arsenal of frostings, sugars, sprinkles, and more to decorate your favorite holiday cookies. The tricks below will ensure your cookies spread the holiday spirit.

THE BEST FROSTING

Royal Icing creates a smooth surface on decorated cookies. It's made with either whipped egg whites or whipped meringue powder, powdered sugar, and water. The addition of just a bit of corn syrup boosts the flavor and helps create a shiny finish. If you want melt-in-your-mouth creamy frosting, use Buttermilk Frosting, which is great for spreading on cookies, cakes, and cupcakes. It's also a yummy filling for sandwich cookies.

ROYAL ICING

TOTAL TIME 10 MINUTES

- 1 (16-ounce) package powdered sugar
- 3 tablespoons meringue powder
- 5 to 6 tablespoons warm water
- 1 teaspoon light corn syrup
- Food coloring paste (optional)

Combine powdered sugar, meringue powder, water, and corn syrup in a large bowl. Beat at medium-low speed with an electric mixer 5 to 7 minutes. Divide and tint with food coloring, if desired. Icing dries quickly, so keep it covered at all times. Makes about 3 cups

BUTTERMILK FROSTING

TOTAL TIME 8 MINUTES

- ½ cup butter, softened
- 1 (16-ounce) package powdered sugar
- 1 teaspoon vanilla extract
- 4 to 5 tablespoons buttermilk

Beat butter at medium speed with an electric mixer until creamy. Gradually add powdered sugar, beating at low speed until blended. Slowly beat in vanilla and 4 tablespoons buttermilk. Increase speed to medium, and beat until smooth. If desired, beat in remaining 1 tablespoon buttermilk, 1 teaspoon at a time, until desired consistency is reached. Makes about 3½ cups

DECORATING WITH ROYAL ICING

Use the tips below when decorating with Royal Icing.

PIPE BORDERS: Use a piping bag or squeeze bottle to pipe the borders and edges of your cookies. Let the icing dry completely, about 20 minutes, before continuing to the next step.

FLOOD: Apply the icing to the surface of the cookie. You don't have to fill every spot. Tilting the cookie will allow the icing to flow into space. A toothpick can help pull it into smaller spaces.

TRIM: You can accent Royal Icing with sanding sugar or colored sprinkles before the icing hardens. Allow the cookies to dry several hours before storing them between sheets of waxed paper.

COLOR: Allow the first color to dry before adding a second color. Colored icing will darken a bit as it sets, so it's best to make the color just a bit lighter than you want. It can then darken to the desired shade.

THIN: After piping edges of the cookies, add a few drops of water to the remaining icing to thin it. If it becomes too thin, mix in a small amount of powdered sugar. If it's too thick, it won't flow over the cookies for a smooth finish. If any air bubbles form on the icing, use a toothpick to gently pop them.

HOW TO FREEZE COOKIES

* Cool unfrosted cookies completely before storing.
* Separate unfrosted cookies with layers of waxed paper.
* Double-bag cookies in zip-top plastic bags for freezing.
* For crisp cookies, bring to room temperature, and then reheat at 325°F for 3 to 5 minutes.

SECRETS OF A CHRISTMAS COOKIE SWAP

Hosting a cookie swap is a great way to multitask, offering you a chance to get together with friends during the busy season and shortcut your holiday baking. Everyone loves holiday cookies, but not everyone has time to bake three or more varieties. Cookie swaps are easy to organize, and everyone goes home with a multitude of treats to celebrate the holiday season. Follow these five simple steps to hosting a successful swap.

1. PLAN EARLY! The holiday season becomes busy, and friends' schedules fill up quickly. People are more likely to attend if you allow for plenty of advance notice.

2. INVITE! Extend the invite to a few more guests than you want to have. Chances are not everyone you invite will be able to attend. Remember to ask attendees to tell you what type of cookie they plan to bring since it's the host's job to keep a running list and (hopefully!) avoid duplicates.

3. SHARE! Ask guests to email you their recipes ahead of time so you can print them on Christmas-themed recipe cards. For a souvenir, bind the cards in a cookie swap cookbook, complete with the date of the party.

4. SNACK! Prepare some savory seasonal snacks and drinks to enjoy. You and your guests will be sampling lots of cookies, so it's nice to offer something to eat to balance the sweets.

5. WRAP IT UP! With all the cookies gathered in one area, provide tins, boxes, and trays for guests to package their goodies together. Don't forget labels! Set out pens, tags, ribbons, and bows for finishing touches. Consider buying festive glass ornaments as a party favor to add an extra-special touch to the wrapped cookies.

ASSEMBLE A SHOWSTOPPING COOKIE PLATTER

Think of your platter like a clock, and you'll have an artful presentation in about a minute.

STEP 1: Begin with the tan and light beige cookies, grouping them at roughly twelve, four, and eight on your imaginary cookie clock.

STEP 2: Next, fill in with brown (dark chocolate) and white (sugared or frosted) cookies in a clockwise pattern to add neutral color.

STEP 3: Fill in the last few open slots with colorful cookies, making sure to balance the platter with pops of color.

STEP 4: Save the prettiest cookies for the prominent spots on the platter. Dot with holiday candies for a final touch.

COOKIES FOR SANTA

Perfect with a glass of milk at midnight, these cookies will treat your sweet tooth — or jolly old Saint Nick's — in a pinch.

WHITE CHOCOLATE–GINGERBREAD STARS

These simple yet elegant cookies will be the star of any holiday cookie tray.

HANDS-ON TIME 1 HOUR   TOTAL TIME 2 HOURS 45 MINUTES   MAKES 28 COOKIES

1   cup packed brown sugar
¾   cup butter, softened
½   cup molasses
1   large egg
3   cups all-purpose flour
2   teaspoons ground ginger
2   teaspoons ground cinnamon
1   teaspoon baking soda
½   teaspoon table salt
½   teaspoon ground cloves
    Cooking spray
1   (4-ounce) white chocolate baking bar, chopped
2   tablespoons coarse white sparkling sugar

1. Beat the brown sugar, butter, molasses, and egg at medium speed with an electric mixer until well blended. Add the flour, ginger, cinnamon, baking soda, salt, and cloves, beating at low speed. Place the dough on a lightly floured surface; shape the dough into a ball, and flatten into a disk. Cover and chill 1 hour or until firm.

2. Preheat the oven to 350°F. Lightly coat large baking sheets with cooking spray. Place the dough on a lightly floured surface, and roll to ¼-inch thickness. Cut with a floured 3- to 4-inch star-shaped cutter, rerolling dough once. Place the cookies 2 inches apart on prepared baking sheets.

3. Bake at 350°F for 10 to 12 minutes or until no indentation remains when touched in center. Transfer to wire racks, and cool completely (about 20 minutes).

4. Microwave the white chocolate, uncovered, in a microwave-safe bowl at HIGH 45 seconds to 1 minute or until smooth. Spoon into a zip-top plastic freezer bag; seal bag. Snip 1 corner of the bag to make a small hole; squeeze the bag to drizzle chocolate over the cookies. Sprinkle with sparkling sugar immediately. Let stand 30 minutes or until set.

TRIPLE GINGERSNAPPERS

Fresh, ground, and crystallized ginger inspired the name of these tasty cookies.

HANDS-ON TIME 1 HOUR 15 MINUTES   TOTAL TIME 6 HOURS 45 MINUTES   MAKES 24 COOKIES

½ cup butter, softened

¾ cup plus 2 tablespoons granulated sugar

2 tablespoons light brown sugar

2 teaspoons dark molasses

1 large egg white

2 tablespoons grated fresh ginger

1⅓ cups all-purpose flour

1 tablespoon ground ginger

1 teaspoon ground cinnamon

½ teaspoon baking soda

¼ teaspoon table salt

¼ teaspoon ground nutmeg

¼ teaspoon ground cloves

⅓ cup crystallized ginger, minced

Plastic wrap

Parchment paper

1. Beat the first 4 ingredients at medium-high speed with an electric mixer 30 seconds. Add the egg white and fresh ginger; beat 1 minute. Sift together the flour and next 6 ingredients. Add the flour mixture to the butter mixture; beat at low speed 30 seconds. Scrape the bowl; fold in the crystallized ginger.

2. Divide the dough into 2 disks; wrap tightly in plastic wrap. Chill 4 hours to 3 days. Unwrap 1 dough disk; generously flour both sides. Place between 2 pieces of parchment paper, and roll to ⅛-inch thickness. Chill 30 minutes. Repeat procedure with remaining dough disk.

3. Line the baking sheets with parchment paper. Cut the chilled dough with a 2½-inch round cutter; place the cookies 2 inches apart on baking sheets. Chill 15 minutes.

4. Preheat the oven to 350°F. Bake, in batches, 12 minutes. Rotate the baking sheets front to back; bake 4 more minutes. (Cookies will puff up and collapse.) Cool completely on parchment paper on wire racks.

THAT'S A WRAP

Heap cookies into tins lined with tissue paper — look for inexpensive retro tins featuring holiday scenes, galvanized tins, or red and silver tins.

WHITE CHOCOLATE–OATMEAL–RAISIN COOKIES

Fiori di Sicilia, an Italian flavoring, gives these easy drop cookies a subtle orange taste.

HANDS-ON TIME 10 MINUTES   TOTAL TIME 1 HOUR 45 MINUTES   MAKES 30 COOKIES

1 cup all-purpose flour
½ teaspoon baking soda
½ teaspoon ground cinnamon
¼ teaspoon table salt
½ cup plus 2 tablespoons unsalted butter, softened
½ cup granulated sugar
½ cup packed light brown sugar
1 large egg
1 teaspoon Fiori di Sicilia or orange extract
1 cup uncooked regular oats
8 ounces white chocolate, chopped (about 2 cups)
½ cup raisins or golden raisins
   Parchment paper

1. Stir together the first 4 ingredients in a medium bowl.

2. Beat the butter at medium speed with an electric mixer until creamy; gradually add the sugars, beating well. Beat in the egg and Fiori di Sicilia just until combined. Add the flour mixture and oats; stir until blended. Stir in the white chocolate and raisins. Cover and chill the dough for 1 hour.

3. Preheat the oven to 350°F. Line 2 large baking sheets with parchment paper. Drop the batter by heaping tablespoonfuls, 3 inches apart, onto prepared baking sheets.

4. Bake at 350°F for 13 to 15 minutes or until lightly browned. Cool on baking sheets 5 minutes. Transfer the cookies to wire racks, and cool completely (about 20 minutes).

WHITE CHOCOLATE-PRETZEL COOKIES

For soft cookies, bake for 10 minutes. For crispy cookies, leave in the oven for 14 minutes.

HANDS-ON TIME 45 MINUTES   TOTAL TIME 45 MINUTES   MAKES 60 COOKIES

Parchment paper
2¼ cups plus 2 tablespoons all-purpose flour
1 teaspoon baking soda
¾ teaspoon table salt
¾ cup butter, softened
¾ cup granulated sugar
¾ cup packed dark brown sugar
2 large eggs
1½ teaspoons vanilla extract
1½ (12-ounce) packages semisweet chocolate morsels
1 (7-ounce) package white chocolate-covered mini-pretzel twists, coarsely crushed

1. Preheat the oven to 350°F. Line baking sheets with parchment paper. Stir together the flour, baking soda, and salt.

2. Beat the butter, granulated sugar, and brown sugar at medium speed with an electric mixer until light and fluffy. Beat in the eggs and vanilla. Gradually add the flour mixture to the butter mixture, beating at low speed just until blended. Stir in the chocolate morsels and pretzels.

3. Drop the dough by tablespoonfuls 1 to 2 inches apart onto prepared baking sheets.

4. Bake at 350°F for 10 to 14 minutes. Immediately transfer to wire racks, and cool completely (about 20 minutes).

PRETZEL-TOFFEE-CHOCOLATE CHUNK COOKIES

Studded with salty pretzels and chocolate-toffee candy, these cookies are quite the treat.

HANDS-ON TIME 28 MINUTES   TOTAL TIME 1 HOUR 38 MINUTES   MAKES ABOUT 36 COOKIES

Parchment paper
- 1 cup butter, softened
- 1 cup packed light brown sugar
- ½ cup granulated sugar
- 1 large egg
- 2 teaspoons vanilla extract
- 2½ cups all-purpose flour
- ¾ teaspoon baking soda
- ¼ teaspoon table salt
- 1½ cups mini-pretzel twists, coarsely crushed
- 4 (1.4-ounce) chocolate-covered toffee candy bars, chopped
- 2 (4-ounce) bittersweet chocolate baking bars, chopped

1. Preheat the oven to 350°F. Line baking sheets with parchment paper. Beat the butter at medium speed with an electric mixer until creamy; gradually add the sugars, beating well. Add the egg and vanilla; beat well.

2. Stir together the flour, baking soda, and salt; gradually add to the butter mixture, beating at low speed after each addition. Stir in the pretzels, toffee candy, and chocolate. Drop the dough by heaping tablespoonfuls 1 inch apart onto prepared baking sheets.

3. Bake at 350°F for 12 to 14 minutes or until golden brown. Cool on baking sheets 5 minutes. Transfer to wire racks, and cool completely (about 20 minutes).

JAVA-TOFFEE COOKIES

Crunchy and sweet with a buttery finish, toffee elevates the coffee flavor in these cookies.

HANDS-ON TIME 1 HOUR 30 MINUTES   TOTAL TIME 9 HOURS 30 MINUTES   MAKES 96 COOKIES

3½ cups all-purpose flour
½ teaspoon baking soda
½ teaspoon table salt
1 cup butter, softened
1½ cups granulated sugar
½ cup packed light brown sugar
3 tablespoons instant coffee granules or crystals
3 teaspoons vanilla extract
2 large eggs
4 (1.4-ounce) bars chocolate-covered English toffee candy, finely chopped
Plastic wrap
Parchment paper

1. Stir together the flour, baking soda, and salt.

2. Beat the butter, granulated sugar, brown sugar, coffee granules, and vanilla at medium speed with an electric mixer until fluffy. Add the eggs, 1 at a time, beating after each addition. Gradually add the flour mixture to the butter mixture, beating at low speed just until blended. Stir in the chopped candy.

3. Shape the dough into 4 (6-inch) logs. Wrap in plastic wrap; chill 8 hours or up to 3 days.

4. Preheat the oven to 350°F. Line baking sheets with parchment paper. Unwrap the dough; cut the logs into ¼-inch slices. Place the slices 1 inch apart on prepared baking sheets. Bake at 350°F for 8 to 12 minutes or until lightly browned. Cool on baking sheets 2 minutes. Transfer to wire racks, and cool completely (about 20 minutes).

THAT'S A WRAP

Keep prepared dough on hand in the refrigerator for a quick and delicious gift during the holidays. Arrange homemade cookies on a festive platter for a holiday party hostess.

CHOCOLATE-CAPPUCCINO COOKIES

Instant coffee deepens the chocolate flavor in these cookies and adds a balance of bitterness.

HANDS-ON TIME 1 HOUR 5 MINUTES   TOTAL TIME 1 HOUR 50 MINUTES   MAKES 96 COOKIES

5½ cups all-purpose flour
1   cup unsweetened baking cocoa
¼   cup instant coffee granules or crystals
1   teaspoon baking powder
1   teaspoon baking soda
1   teaspoon table salt
2   cups butter, softened
4   cups packed light brown sugar
4   large eggs
1   (10-ounce) package cinnamon-flavored baking chips
    Cooking spray

1. Preheat the oven to 350°F. Stir together the flour, cocoa, coffee granules, baking powder, baking soda, and salt.

2. Beat the butter at medium speed with an electric mixer until creamy. Gradually add the brown sugar, beating well. Beat in the eggs.

3. Gradually add the flour mixture to the butter mixture, beating at low speed just until blended. Stir in the cinnamon chips. Drop the dough by rounded tablespoonfuls 2 inches apart onto baking sheets coated with cooking spray.

4. Bake at 350°F for 8 to 10 minutes. Cool on baking sheet 5 minutes. Transfer to wire racks, and cool completely (about 20 minutes).

CHOCOLATE-CHERRY SUGAR-CRUSTED SHORTBREAD

Ideal for gifting, these bite-size treats can be packed in a basket for a holiday party hostess.

HANDS-ON TIME 10 MINUTES   TOTAL TIME 48 MINUTES   MAKES 64 COOKIES

1	cup butter, softened
½	cup powdered sugar
2½	cups all-purpose flour
⅛	teaspoon table salt
¼	cup semisweet chocolate mini-morsels
¼	cup dried cherries, finely chopped
1	teaspoon vanilla extract
	Aluminum foil
	Cooking spray
1	tablespoon granulated sugar
½	cup granulated sugar

1. Preheat the oven to 325°F. Beat the butter at medium speed with an electric mixer until creamy; add the powdered sugar, beating well.

2. Stir together the flour and salt; gradually add to the butter mixture, beating until well blended. Stir in the chocolate mini-morsels, cherries, and vanilla.

3. Line an 8-inch square pan with aluminum foil, allowing the foil to extend over the edges of the pan. Lightly coat the foil with cooking spray, and sprinkle with 1 tablespoon granulated sugar. Press the dough into the pan.

4. Bake at 325°F for 40 minutes or until golden. Cool 30 minutes or until slightly warm in the pan. Use the foil to gently lift the shortbread from the pan. Gently remove the foil. Cut the shortbread into 1-inch squares using a sharp knife. Place ½ cup granulated sugar in a small bowl. Roll the shortbread squares in the sugar.

CHOCOLATE-COVERED CHERRY COOKIES

Place each of these cookies in a candy cup, and gift them in a holiday-themed box.

HANDS-ON TIME 20 MINUTES　　TOTAL TIME 2 HOURS 35 MINUTES　　MAKES 30 COOKIES

½　cup butter, softened
1　cup sugar
1　large egg
1　tablespoon kirsch (optional)
1½　cups all-purpose flour
½　cup unsweetened baking cocoa
¼　teaspoon baking powder
¼　teaspoon baking soda
¼　teaspoon table salt
　　Plastic wrap
　　Parchment paper
30　chocolate-covered cherries
4　ounces white chocolate baking bars or squares, chopped

1. Beat the butter and sugar at medium speed with an electric mixer until light and fluffy. Add the egg and, if desired, kirsch; beat until blended. Stir together the flour and next 4 ingredients. Beat in the flour mixture on low speed until blended. Wrap the dough in plastic wrap; chill 1 hour.

2. Preheat the oven to 350°F. Line baking sheets with parchment paper. Unwrap the dough; shape into 30 (1-inch) balls. Place the balls 2 inches apart on prepared baking sheets. Bake at 350°F for 10 to 12 minutes or until set. Immediately press 1 chocolate-covered cherry into the center of each cookie. Cool on baking sheets 1 minute. Transfer to wire racks, and cool completely (about 20 minutes).

3. Microwave the white chocolate, uncovered, in a small microwave-safe bowl at HIGH 1 to 2 minutes or until softened and the chocolate can be stirred smooth. Spoon the melted chocolate into a small zip-top plastic freezer bag; seal bag. Snip 1 corner of the bag to make a small hole; squeeze the bag to drizzle chocolate over the cookies. Let stand 30 minutes or until set.

CHERRY-LEMON CANDY CANES

Cherry juice adds tartness to this powdered sugar frosting.

HANDS-ON TIME 18 MINUTES   TOTAL TIME 3 HOURS 4 MINUTES   MAKES 30 COOKIES

1   cup butter, softened
2½   cups powdered sugar
1   large egg
1   tablespoon grated lemon rind
1   teaspoon vanilla extract
2½   cups all-purpose flour
¾   cup dried cherries, chopped
     Plastic wrap
3   tablespoons cherry juice
½   teaspoon red liquid food
     coloring

1. Beat the butter at medium speed with an electric mixer until creamy. Add 1 cup of the powdered sugar, beating until light and fluffy. Add the egg, lemon rind, and vanilla; beat until blended. Gradually add the flour, beating until blended. Stir in the cherries. Wrap the dough in plastic wrap, and chill 2 hours.

2. Preheat the oven to 375°F. Shape the dough into 30 (5- x ½-inch) ropes. Place 2 inches apart on ungreased baking sheets; bend the tops of the ropes over to look like candy canes.

3. Bake at 375°F for 10 to 12 minutes or until the edges of the cookies begin to brown. Cool on baking sheets 2 minutes. Transfer to wire racks, and cool completely (about 20 minutes).

4. Whisk together the cherry juice, food coloring, and the remaining 1½ cups powdered sugar in a small bowl until smooth. Spoon into a zip-top plastic freezer bag; seal bag. Snip 1 corner of the bag to make a small hole; squeeze the bag to drizzle icing over the cookies. Let stand 30 minutes or until set.

* INGREDIENT SWAP *

Don't have cherry juice on hand?
Substitute milk, and increase the
red food coloring as needed.

PEPPERMINT COOKIE CANES

Keep the dough covered with plastic wrap so it won't dry out while rolling the cookies.

HANDS-ON TIME 1 HOUR   TOTAL TIME 1 HOUR 45 MINUTES   MAKES 48 COOKIES

3½   cups cake flour, sifted
1½   teaspoons baking powder
¼   teaspoon table salt
½   cup butter, softened
½   cup butter-flavored shortening
      or regular shortening
1½   cups sugar
1   large egg
1½   teaspoons peppermint
      extract
½   teaspoon vanilla extract
¾   teaspoon red food
      coloring paste

1. Stir together the flour, baking powder, and salt.

2. Beat the butter and shortening at medium speed with an electric mixer until creamy; gradually add the sugar, beating well. Add the egg, beating well. Stir in the peppermint extract and vanilla. Gradually add the flour mixture, beating until blended. Remove half of the dough from the bowl. Add the red food coloring to the dough in the bowl; mix until the coloring is evenly distributed.

3. Working with half of the dough at a time, shape the plain dough by teaspoonfuls into 4-inch-long ropes; place 2 inches apart on ungreased baking sheets. (Keep plain dough ropes covered.) Repeat with the red dough. For each cookie, place 1 red rope and 1 plain rope side by side; carefully twist together. Roll the twisted ropes into 1 smooth rope. Shape the rope into a cane; twist as needed to complete the stripe design. Chill 15 minutes.

4. Preheat the oven to 375°F. Bake at 375°F for 10 to 12 minutes or until light golden brown. Cool on baking sheets 2 minutes. Transfer to wire racks, and cool completely (about 20 minutes).

SPARKLING GINGER STARS

A heavy sugar crust and peppery bite of fresh ginger make these cookies scrumptious.

HANDS-ON TIME 12 MINUTES   TOTAL TIME 3 HOURS   MAKES 24 COOKIES

1½   cups all-purpose flour
½   teaspoon baking soda
½   teaspoon table salt
2   teaspoons ground ginger
1   teaspoon ground cinnamon
¼   teaspoon ground cloves
¼   teaspoon freshly grated
     nutmeg
½   cup unsalted butter, softened
½   cup firmly packed dark
     brown sugar
¼   cup dark molasses
1   large egg yolk
1   tablespoon grated lemon rind
1   tablespoon grated
     fresh ginger
½   teaspoon vanilla extract
     Plastic wrap
     Parchment paper
1   large egg
2   tablespoons whipping cream
1   (3.25-ounce) jar coarse
     sparkling sugar

1. Stir together the first 7 ingredients until blended.

2. Beat the butter at medium speed with an electric mixer until creamy; gradually add the brown sugar, beating well. Add the molasses and next 4 ingredients, beating well. Gradually add the flour mixture, beating just until blended after each addition.

3. Shape the dough into a ball, and divide it in half. Flatten each half into a round disk; wrap each in plastic wrap, and chill 2½ hours until firm.

4. Preheat the oven to 325°F. Line baking sheets with parchment paper. Place the dough on a lightly floured surface, and roll out the dough, 1 portion at a time, to ¼-inch thickness. Cut into star shapes, using a floured 4-inch cookie cutter. Place ½-inch apart on prepared baking sheets.

5. Whisk together 1 egg and whipping cream; brush the egg wash lightly over the cookies. Sprinkle heavily with the sparkling sugar.

6. Bake at 325°F for 17 minutes or until the cookies are puffed and slightly darker around the edges. Cool 2 minutes on baking sheets. Transfer to wire racks, and cool completely (about 20 minutes).

THAT'S A WRAP

Inside a wide juice glass, pile cookies high. Then include a gift tag that suggests filling the glass with milk for dunking.

HONEY-ORANGE-GINGER COOKIES

Honey adds floral notes balanced by the extra zing of orange and ginger.

HANDS-ON TIME 40 MINUTES   TOTAL TIME 1 HOUR 10 MINUTES   MAKES 48 COOKIES

2¼ cups all-purpose flour
1 tablespoon grated orange rind
1 teaspoon ground ginger
½ teaspoon baking soda
½ teaspoon baking powder
½ cup butter, softened
⅔ cup sugar
½ cup honey
1 teaspoon orange extract
1 large egg
Additional sugar

1. Stir together the flour, orange rind, ginger, baking soda, and baking powder. Beat the butter and ⅔ cup sugar at medium speed with an electric mixer until creamy. Add the honey, orange extract, and egg; beat until blended. Gradually add the flour mixture to the butter mixture, beating at low speed just until blended. Cover the dough, and chill 30 minutes to 1 hour.

2. Preheat the oven to 350°F. Shape the dough into 48 (1-inch) balls. Place the additional sugar in a bowl. Roll the balls in the sugar. Place the balls 2 inches apart on ungreased baking sheets. Flatten the balls slightly with the bottom of a glass.

3. Bake at 350°F for 8 to 10 minutes or until lightly browned. Cool on baking sheets 2 minutes. Transfer to wire racks, and cool completely (about 20 minutes).

GINGER-CRANBERRY COOKIES

Substitute another dried fruit if you don't have dried cranberries on hand.

HANDS-ON TIME 20 MINUTES   TOTAL TIME 1 HOUR 5 MINUTES   MAKES 36 COOKIES

Parchment paper
- 1 cup butter, softened
- ¾ cup granulated sugar
- ¾ cup firmly packed light brown sugar
- 1 large egg
- 2¼ cups all-purpose flour
- 1 teaspoon baking soda
- ½ teaspoon table salt
- 1½ cups sweetened dried cranberries
- ¼ cup crystallized ginger, finely chopped

1. Preheat the oven to 375°F. Line baking sheets with parchment paper. Beat the butter at medium speed with an electric mixer until creamy. Add both of the sugars; beat 2 minutes. Beat in the egg until blended. Stir in the flour, baking soda, and salt. (Dough will be crumbly.) Stir in the cranberries and ginger.

2. Drop the dough by rounded tablespoonfuls 2 inches apart onto prepared baking sheets.

3. Bake at 375°F for 10 to 11 minutes or until light golden brown. (Centers will be soft.) Cool 1 minute on baking sheets. Transfer to wire racks, and cool completely (about 20 minutes).

✳ COOKIE ROOKIE ✳
This dough is slightly crumbly.
Press together spoonfuls of dough, and
place them on the baking sheet.

CRANBERRY-ORANGE-WALNUT COOKIES

Fresh zest accentuates the orange flavor in the glaze drizzled on these delightful cookies.

HANDS-ON TIME 25 MINUTES   TOTAL TIME 50 MINUTES   MAKES 20 COOKIES

1   (16-ounce) package ready-to-bake refrigerated sugar cookies
½   cup chopped walnuts, toasted
¼   cup sweetened dried cranberries, chopped
1½   teaspoons grated orange rind
    Cooking spray
1   cup powdered sugar
4   teaspoons fresh orange juice

1. Preheat the oven to 350°F. Stir together the cookie dough, walnuts, cranberries, and orange rind with a wooden spoon, or knead with hands until well blended. Drop the dough by rounded tablespoonfuls 2 inches apart onto baking sheets coated with cooking spray.

2. Bake at 350°F for 13 to 15 minutes or until the edges are set. Cool on baking sheets 2 minutes. Transfer to wire racks, and cool completely (about 20 minutes).

3. Stir together the powdered sugar and orange juice until smooth. Spoon into a zip-top plastic freezer bag; seal the bag. Snip 1 corner of the bag to make a small hole; squeeze the bag to drizzle icing over the cookies. Let stand 30 minutes or until set.

> ✳ **COOKIE ROOKIE** ✳
> To toast walnuts, spread the nuts in an ungreased shallow pan. Bake at 350°F for 6 to 10 minutes, stirring occasionally, until light brown.

CRANBERRY-WALNUT SHORTBREAD

Tangy cranberries, semisweet chocolate, and nuts are packed into each buttery bite.

HANDS-ON TIME 15 MINUTES   TOTAL TIME 1 HOUR 55 MINUTES   MAKES 24 COOKIES

Aluminum foil
Cooking spray
1   cup butter, softened
½   cup powdered sugar
2½ cups all-purpose flour
Dash of table salt
¼   cup finely chopped walnuts
¼   cup finely chopped sweetened dried cranberries
1   teaspoon vanilla extract
½   cup semisweet chocolate morsels
2   tablespoons shortening
Coarsely chopped walnuts

1. Preheat the oven to 325°F. Line the bottom and sides of an 8-inch square pan with aluminum foil, allowing 2 to 3 inches to extend over the sides. Lightly coat the foil with cooking spray.

2. Beat the butter at medium speed with an electric mixer until creamy. Add the powdered sugar; beat well. Add the flour and salt, beating until well blended. Stir in the walnuts, cranberries, and vanilla. Press the dough into the pan.

3. Bake at 325°F for 40 minutes or until golden. Cool in the pan 30 minutes. Lift the shortbread from the pan, using the foil sides as handles. Gently remove the foil.

4. Microwave the chocolate morsels and 2 tablespoons shortening in a small microwave-safe bowl at HIGH for 1 to 1½ minutes, stirring once, until softened and the chocolate can be stirred smooth. Drizzle chocolate over shortbread. Sprinkle the chopped walnuts on top. Let stand until set (about 30 minutes). Cut into squares using a sharp knife.

THAT'S A WRAP

For a yummy, easy-to-package gift, cut shortbread into bite-size pieces, place in a cellophane treat bag, and tie with a festive holiday ribbon.

WREATH MACAROONS

To shape the center of the cookie, use your fingers. This is a great way to involve kids!

HANDS-ON TIME 30 MINUTES   TOTAL TIME 1 HOUR 15 MINUTES   MAKES 36 COOKIES

Parchment paper
14 ounces sweetened flaked coconut
2 large egg whites
½ cup plus 2 teaspoons sugar
1 teaspoon vanilla extract
Holiday nonpareils
Finely chopped candied red and green cherries

1. Preheat the oven to 350°F. Line 3 baking sheets with parchment paper. Stir together the coconut, egg whites, sugar, and vanilla. Drop by heaping tablespoonfuls onto prepared baking sheets, about 12 per sheet. Make a hole in the center of each cookie; pinch each cookie into a wreath shape. Sprinkle with nonpareils and cherries.

2. Bake 2 baking sheets at 350°F for 14 minutes. Rotate the pans front to back, and bake 2 more minutes or until the coconut begins to brown. Cool the cookies on parchment paper on wire racks; cool completely (about 20 minutes). Repeat with the remaining baking sheet.

> ✳ **COOKIE ROOKIE** ✳
> Egg whites will have better volume when beaten if the eggs are kept in a bowl of warm water for 10 minutes beforehand.

COCONUT-MACADAMIA SHORTBREAD

Keep a log of this cookie dough in the freezer to bake up when company is coming.

HANDS-ON TIME 22 MINUTES   TOTAL TIME 4 HOURS 30 MINUTES   MAKES 48 COOKIES

2 cups all-purpose flour
¼ teaspoon baking powder
⅛ teaspoon table salt
1 cup butter, softened
¾ cup powdered sugar
2 teaspoons vanilla extract
¼ teaspoon coconut extract
1 cup flaked sweetened coconut, toasted
½ cup finely chopped macadamia nuts
  Waxed paper
  Parchment paper or cooking spray

1. Stir together the flour, baking powder, and salt.

2. Beat the butter at medium speed with an electric mixer until creamy. Gradually add the powdered sugar, beating until smooth. Stir in the vanilla and coconut extract until blended. Gradually add the flour mixture to the butter mixture, beating at low speed just until blended. Stir in the coconut and nuts.

3. Shape the dough into 2 (7-inch) logs; wrap in waxed paper. Chill 4 hours.

4. Preheat the oven to 350°F. Line baking sheets with parchment paper or coat with cooking spray. Unwrap the dough; cut each log into 24 slices. Place the slices 1 inch apart on prepared baking sheets.

5. Bake at 350°F for 10 to 12 minutes or until edges are golden. Cool on baking sheets 2 minutes. Transfer to wire racks, and cool completely (about 20 minutes).

✳ COOKIE ROOKIE ✳

All nuts should be stored in the refrigerator or freezer because they have a high fat content and can go rancid when exposed to light and heat.

CANDY BAR SUGAR COOKIES

Customize these easy sugar cookies for guests by using their favorite candy bars.

HANDS-ON TIME 30 MINUTES   TOTAL TIME 1 HOUR 20 MINUTES   MAKES 48 COOKIES

Parchment paper
½ cup shortening
¼ cup butter, softened
½ cup firmly packed light brown sugar
1 large egg
1½ teaspoons vanilla extract
2 cups all-purpose flour
1½ teaspoons baking powder
½ teaspoons baking soda
½ teaspoon table salt
2 (2.1-ounce) chocolate-covered crispy peanut-buttery candy bars, coarsely chopped
6 tablespoons turbinado sugar

1. Preheat the oven to 375°F. Line baking sheets with parchment paper. Beat the shortening and butter at medium speed with an electric mixer until light and fluffy. Gradually add the brown sugar, beating until smooth. Add the egg and vanilla, beating until blended.

2. Stir together the flour and next 3 ingredients; gradually add to the shortening mixture, beating just until blended. Stir in the candy. Place the turbinado sugar in a small bowl. Shape the dough into 1-inch balls; roll each ball in sugar. Place the balls 3 inches apart on prepared baking sheets.

3. Bake at 375°F for 9 to 10 minutes or until lightly browned. Cool 2 minutes on baking sheets Transfer to wire racks, and cool completely (about 20 minutes).

> ✳ **COOKIE ROOKIE** ✳
> When baking many batches of cookies, place the dough onto sheets of parchment paper, assembly-line fashion. Then slide each batch on a baking sheet when ready to bake. Using parchment paper eliminates the need to grease the baking sheets.

HIDDEN KISS COOKIES

Use candy cane kisses to add a fun peppermint twist to your holiday cookie tray.

HANDS-ON TIME 1 HOUR   TOTAL TIME 1 HOUR 30 MINUTES   MAKES 42 COOKIES

Parchment paper
2¼ cups all-purpose flour
1 cup sliced almonds
⅔ cup powdered sugar
½ teaspoon table salt
1¼ cups butter, softened
1 teaspoon vanilla extract
¼ teaspoon almond extract
42 chocolate kisses
Additional powdered sugar

1. Preheat the oven to 350°F. Line 2 baking sheets with parchment paper. Pulse the flour, almonds, ⅔ cup powdered sugar, and salt in a food processor until the almonds are finely ground.

2. Beat the butter, vanilla, and almond extract at medium-high speed with an electric mixer about 30 seconds or until creamy. Add the flour mixture in 2 batches, beating until blended after each addition. Turn the dough out onto a lightly floured surface, and knead 4 to 5 times. Divide the dough in half.

3. Working with 1 dough portion, drop by heaping teaspoonfuls 1 inch apart onto prepared baking sheets. Press 1 chocolate kiss into center of each cookie. Working with the remaining dough portion, cover each chocolate kiss with another heaping teaspoonful of dough. Pinch the top and bottom edges of the dough together to seal.

4. Bake at 350°F for 15 minutes, placing 1 baking sheet on the middle oven rack and 1 sheet on the lower oven rack. Rotate the pans front to back and top rack to bottom rack. Bake 3 to 5 more minutes or until the edges of the cookies just begin to brown. Cool the cookies on parchment paper on wire racks 10 minutes. Sprinkle with additional powdered sugar.

> **❋ INGREDIENT SWAP ❋**
> Vary the treasures in your cookies! Instead of kisses, try candied cherries, malted milk balls, caramels, or gummy fruit candies.

SNICKERDOODLE SPRITZ COOKIES

Avoid over-developing the dough when mixing. It results in a tough cookie.

HANDS-ON TIME 1 HOUR TOTAL TIME 1 HOUR MAKES 72 COOKIES

1 cup powdered sugar
1 cup butter, softened
1 teaspoon vanilla extract
1 large egg
2 cups all-purpose flour
½ teaspoon table salt
¼ cup granulated sugar
1 tablespoon ground
   cinnamon

1. Preheat the oven to 375°F. Beat the powdered sugar and butter at medium speed with an electric mixer until light and fluffy. Add the vanilla and egg; beat until blended. Add the flour and salt, and beat until well blended.

2. Fit a cookie press with the desired template. Fill the cookie press; press the dough onto ungreased baking sheets. Stir together the granulated sugar and cinnamon in a small bowl; sprinkle over the cookies.

3. Bake at 375°F for 7 to 9 minutes or until the edges are light golden. Cool 5 minutes on baking sheets. Transfer to wire racks, and cool completely (about 20 minutes).

> **✳ COOKIE ROOKIE ✳**
> It's important to use ungreased baking sheets when squeezing dough from a cookie press so the dough releases from the press and adheres to the sheets.

HOLIDAY SNICKERDOODLES

Pillowy with a sweet tang, these sprinkled treats are the quintessential holiday cookie.

HANDS-ON TIME 45 MINUTES   TOTAL TIME 45 MINUTES   MAKES 42 COOKIES

Parchment paper
2¾ cups all-purpose flour
1½ teaspoons cream of tartar
1   teaspoon baking soda
¼   teaspoon table salt
2   teaspoons ground cinnamon
1   cup butter, softened
1⅓ cups granulated sugar
2   large eggs
¼   cup green sanding sugar
¼   cup red sanding sugar

1. Preheat the oven to 400°F. Line baking sheets with parchment paper.

2. Stir together the flour, cream of tartar, baking soda, salt, and 1 teaspoon of the cinnamon.

3. Beat the butter and granulated sugar at medium speed with an electric mixer until light and fluffy. Beat in the eggs. Gradually add the flour mixture to the butter mixture, beating at low speed just until blended.

4. Stir together green sanding sugar and ½ teaspoon of the cinnamon in a small bowl. Stir together the red sanding sugar and remaining ½ teaspoon cinnamon in another small bowl.

5. Shape the dough into 1¼-inch balls. Roll half of the balls in the green sugar mixture; roll the remaining balls in the red sugar mixture. Place the balls 2 inches apart on prepared baking sheets.

6. Bake at 400°F for 12 to 14 minutes or until set. Cool on baking sheets 2 minutes. Transfer to wire racks, and cool completely (about 20 minutes).

> ✳ INGREDIENT SWAP ✳
> For traditional snickerdoodles, use granulated sugar instead of the red and green decorating sugars.

EASIEST PEANUT BUTTER COOKIES

This 4-ingredient cookie features a signature pattern created with the tines of a fork.

HANDS-ON TIME 20 MINUTES   TOTAL TIME 35 MINUTES   MAKES ABOUT 30 COOKIES

1   cup peanut butter
1   cup sugar
1   large egg
1   teaspoon vanilla extract

1. Preheat the oven to 325°F. Stir together the peanut butter, sugar, egg, and vanilla in a large bowl until blended. Shape the dough into 1-inch balls. Place the balls, 1 inch apart, on ungreased baking sheets, and flatten gently with the tines of a fork.

2. Bake at 325°F for 15 minutes or until golden brown. Transfer to wire racks, and cool completely (about 20 minutes).

✳ INGREDIENT SWAP ✳
If you don't have peanut butter in the pantry, almond butter or any other nut butter will work, too.

BROWNIE COOKIES

These double-chocolate cookies are similar in texture to a thick, fudgy brownie.

HANDS-ON TIME 1 HOUR   TOTAL TIME 1 HOUR   MAKES 30 COOKIES

Parchment paper
- ½ cup butter, cut into pieces
- 4 ounces unsweetened baking chocolate, chopped
- 3 cups semisweet chocolate morsels, divided
- 1½ cups all-purpose flour
- ½ teaspoon baking powder
- ½ teaspoon table salt
- 4 large eggs
- 1½ cups sugar
- 2 teaspoons vanilla extract
- 2 cups chopped toasted pecans

1. Preheat the oven to 350°F. Line baking sheets with parchment paper. Combine the butter, baking chocolate, and 1½ cups of the chocolate morsels in a heavy saucepan. Cook over low, stirring constantly, until the butter and chocolate are melted. Remove from heat; cool completely.

2. Stir together the flour, baking powder, and salt. Beat the eggs, sugar, and vanilla at high speed with an electric mixer until well blended. Gradually add the flour mixture, beating at low speed. Add the chocolate mixture, and continue to beat well. Stir in the toasted pecans and the remaining 1½ cups chocolate morsels.

3. Drop the dough by 2 tablespoonfuls 1 inch apart onto prepared baking sheets. Bake at 350°F for 10 minutes. Cool on baking sheets 2 minutes. Transfer to wire racks and cool completely (20 minutes).

THAT'S A WRAP
Use a festive stencil design, and sprinkle powdered sugar on top of these cookies to dress them up for the holidays.

MISSISSIPPI MUD MEDALLIONS

Substitute mini marshmallows for the espresso beans for a kid-friendly version.

HANDS-ON TIME 25 MINUTES   TOTAL TIME 40 MINUTES   MAKES 36 COOKIES

Parchment paper

6   whole graham crackers, divided

2   cups semisweet chocolate morsels

⅔   cup pecan halves, toasted

36   chocolate-covered espresso beans (about ½ cup)

1. Line a baking sheet with parchment paper. Place 3 whole graham crackers in a zip-top plastic freezer bag, and roll with a rolling pin until finely crushed. Spoon the crushed graham crackers by level ½ teaspoonfuls 1 inch apart onto a baking sheet; flatten the crumbs into 1-inch rounds. Break the remaining 3 crackers into ½-inch pieces.

2. Microwave the chocolate morsels in a microwave-safe bowl at HIGH for 30 seconds; stir. Microwave for 10 to 20 more seconds or until melted and smooth, stirring at 10-second intervals.

3. Spoon the melted chocolate into a large zip-top plastic freezer bag. Snip 1 corner of the bag to make a small hole. Pipe the chocolate over each graham cracker round.

4. Working quickly, press 1 (½-inch) graham cracker piece, 1 toasted pecan, and 1 espresso bean onto each chocolate round. Chill 15 minutes. Store in an airtight container at room temperature up to 1 week.

> ✳ **COOKIE ROOKIE** ✳
>
> To transfer the chocolate into a zip-top plastic freezer bag, nestle the corner of the bag in a 1-cup measuring cup, and scrape the melted chocolate into the opened bag. The chocolate will pool in the bottom corner inside the measuring cup and be ready to use immediately.

DECORATED COOKIES

Cutouts are a staple during the holidays. With icings, sugars, candies, and a few helping hands, you can bring these cookies to life.

SPICED SORGHUM SNOWFLAKES

These beautiful cookies are flavored with sweet sorghum and gingerbread spices.

HANDS-ON TIME 3 HOURS 25 MINUTES   TOTAL TIME 5 HOURS 25 MINUTES   MAKES 84 COOKIES

½ cup butter, softened
¼ cup granulated sugar
¼ cup firmly packed dark brown sugar
2 teaspoons grated orange rind
1 large egg
3 tablespoons hot water
1 teaspoon baking soda
½ cup sorghum
3 cups all-purpose flour
2 teaspoons ground ginger
1 teaspoon ground cinnamon
½ teaspoon ground allspice
¼ teaspoon ground nutmeg
¼ teaspoon table salt
   Parchment paper
1 recipe Royal Icing (page 8)
   White sparkling sugar, nonpareils, sugar pearls

1. Beat the butter and sugars at medium speed with a heavy-duty electric stand mixer until fluffy. Add the orange rind and egg, beating until smooth.

2. Stir together the hot water and baking soda in a small bowl until the baking soda is dissolved. Stir in the sorghum.

3. Stir together the flour and next 5 ingredients; add to the butter mixture alternately with the sorghum mixture, beginning and ending with the flour mixture.

4. Divide the dough into 2 equal portions; flatten each into a disk. Cover and chill at least 1 hour or until firm.

5. Preheat the oven to 325°F. Line baking sheets with parchment paper. Place 1 portion of the dough on a lightly floured surface, and roll to ¼-inch thickness. Cut with assorted sizes of floured snowflake-shaped cutters. Place the cutouts, 1 inch apart, on prepared baking sheets. Repeat the procedure with the remaining dough disk. Freeze the cutouts for about 10 minutes.

6. Bake at 325°F for 13 to 15 minutes or until the cookies are puffed and slightly darker around the edges. Cool on the pans for 1 minute. Transfer to wire racks, and cool completely (about 20 minutes).

7. Make Royal Icing. Spoon the icing into a zip-top plastic freezer bag. Snip 1 corner of the bag to make a small hole. Pipe the icing in decorative designs on each cookie. Sprinkle with white sparkling sugar, and decorate with nonpareils and sugar pearls. Let the icing harden at least 1 hour before storing or serving.

> ✳ **INGREDIENT SWAP** ✳
>
> Sorghum is a wonderful sweetener for baked goods. It is a clear, amber-colored liquid with a slightly earthy flavor. If you do not have it on hand, molasses, honey, or maple syrup can be substituted.

SNOW GLOBE COOKIES

For expert tips for decorating cookies, refer to our decorating guide on page 9.

HANDS-ON TIME 1 HOUR   TOTAL TIME 3 HOURS 45 MINUTES   MAKES 8 TO 10 COOKIES

¾ cup butter, softened
¾ cup firmly packed light brown sugar
¾ cup molasses
¼ teaspoon table salt
2 teaspoons ground cinnamon
2 teaspoons ground ginger
¼ teaspoon ground allspice
¼ teaspoon ground cardamom
1 large egg
3½ cups all-purpose flour
1 teaspoon baking powder
½ teaspoon baking soda
   Parchment paper
1 recipe Royal Icing (page 8)
   Blue, green, red, yellow food coloring paste
   White nonpareils, yellow stars, red sanding sugar

1. Melt the butter in a saucepan over low; whisk in brown sugar and next 6 ingredients. Place the mixture in the bowl of a electric stand mixer; let stand 30 minutes. Add egg, beating at low speed just until blended.

2. Stir together the flour, baking powder, and baking soda in a medium bowl; gradually add to the butter mixture, beating at low speed just until blended.

3. Preheat the oven to 350°F. Line baking sheets with parchment paper. On a lightly floured surface, roll the dough to ¼-inch thickness. Cut with a 4-inch snow globe cutter, reserving the remaining dough. Place the cookies 1 inch apart on prepared baking sheets. Create other desired shapes, like mini gingerbread men and trees, using mini cutters and the remaining dough. Place the shapes 1 inch apart on a separate baking sheet.

4. Bake the snow globe cookies at 350°F for 10 to 12 minutes or until lightly browned. Let stand 5 minutes. Transfer to wire racks, and cool completely (about 20 minutes). Bake the mini gingerbread men, snowmen, and tree cookies for 6 to 8 minutes or until lightly browned. Let stand 5 minutes. Transfer to wire racks, and cool completely (about 20 minutes).

5. Make Royal Icing. Separate the icing into 5 bowls. Add blue, green, red, and yellow food coloring to each of 4 bowls, one color icing to each bowl, leaving one bowl for plain white. Spoon each color icing into individual zip-top plastic freezer bags.

6. Snip 1 corner of each icing bag to create a small hole. Squeeze the bag to decorate using white icing to create the snow. Add white nonpareils, and let stand 10 minutes. Fill in the rest of the globe with blue icing, and place the gingerbread men or tree cookies on top, while the icing is still wet. Decorate the gingerbread men and tree cookies with icing and yellow stars. Sprinkle white nonpareils for falling snow effect; let stand 10 minutes. Add red icing to the base, sprinkle with red sanding sugar, and decorate with icing. Let the decorated cookies harden for 1 hour before serving or storing.

STOCKING SUGAR COOKIES

Using sturdy cookie cutters with sharp edges ensures that cookies will keep their shape.

HANDS-ON TIME 1 HOUR   TOTAL TIME 3 HOURS 15 MINUTES   MAKES 30 COOKIES

2½ cups all-purpose flour
1 teaspoon baking powder
¼ teaspoon table salt
¾ cup butter, softened
1 cup granulated sugar
2 large eggs
½ teaspoon vanilla extract
¼ teaspoon almond extract
Plastic wrap
1 (7-ounce) pouch red cookie decorating icing
1 (7-ounce) pouch green cookie decorating icing
1 (7-ounce) pouch white cookie decorating icing
Red, green, and white sanding sugar

1. Stir together the flour, baking powder, and salt in a medium bowl; set aside. Beat the butter and granulated sugar at medium speed with an electric mixer until smooth. Beat in the eggs, one at a time, until blended. Beat in the vanilla and almond extract. Beat in the flour mixture at low speed just until blended. Shape the dough into a ball; wrap in plastic wrap. Chill for 2 hours or until firm.

2. Preheat the oven to 375°F. Unwrap the dough. Roll out the dough on a lightly floured surface to ¼-inch thickness. Cut the dough with a floured 3-inch stocking-shaped cookie cutter. Place the cutouts 1 inch apart on ungreased baking sheets.

3. Bake at 375°F for 10 to 12 minutes or until set. Cool on the baking sheets for 2 minutes. Transfer to wire racks, and cool completely (about 20 minutes).

4. Decorate the cookies using red, green, and white icing and sanding sugar.

THAT'S A WRAP
When tying a ribbon on a cookie gift, attach a festive cookie cutter to the package as an extra keepsake.

SANTA BELL COOKIES

Transform a bell-shaped cookie into cheery Kris Kringle with assorted candies.

HANDS-ON TIME 45 MINUTES   TOTAL TIME 2 HOURS 20 MINUTES   MAKES 12 COOKIES

1   (17.5-ounce) pouch sugar cookie mix
½   cup butter, softened
1   tablespoon all-purpose flour
1   large egg
½   teaspoon almond extract
    Plastic wrap
1   (7-ounce) pouch white cookie decorating icing
½   cup sweetened flaked coconut
2   tablespoons red decorating icing
1   tablespoon brown decorating icing
2   tablespoons coarse red sparkling sugar
24 brown candy-coated milk chocolate candies
12 red cinnamon candies

1. Stir together the cookie mix and next 4 ingredients until a soft dough forms. Shape the dough into a ball; flatten slightly. Wrap in plastic wrap; chill for 1 hour.

2. Preheat the oven to 375°F. Unwrap the dough. Place the dough on a floured surface, and roll to ¼-inch thickness. Cut with a floured 4¾-inch bell-shaped cookie cutter. Place the cutouts 2 inches apart on ungreased baking sheets. Bake at 375°F for 10 to 12 minutes or until the edges are lightly browned. Cool for 2 minutes on baking sheets; transfer to wire racks, and cool completely (about 20 minutes).

3. For each cookie, spread or pipe the white icing onto the bottom of the bell for beard and mustache and onto the top of the bell for the hat pom-pom; sprinkle with coconut. Pipe the red icing under the pom-pom for the hat; sprinkle with red sugar. Use the white icing to attach the milk chocolate candies for the eyes and cinnamon candies for the nose. Use the red icing for the mouth and the brown icing for the eyebrows. Let stand for 30 minutes or until set.

NOTE: We tested with M&Ms.

SNOWMAN COOKIES

Sparkling sugars give these frosted treats an extra shimmering touch.

HANDS-ON TIME 40 MINUTES   TOTAL TIME 1 HOUR 20 MINUTES   MAKES 24 COOKIES

1   (16.5-ounce) package refrigerated sugar cookie dough
¼   cup all-purpose flour
1   (7-ounce) pouch white cookie decorating icing
      White and black sparkling sugar
1   (7-ounce) pouch green cookie decorating icing
1   (7-ounce) pouch blue cookie decorating icing
1   (4.25-ounce) tube black decorating icing
1   (4.25-ounce) tube red decorating icing
24   snowflake candy sprinkles
1   ounce orange fondant
72   red cinnamon candies
      Waxed paper or aluminum foil

1. Preheat the oven to 375°F. Break up the cookie dough into a medium bowl. Knead in the flour until well blended.

2. Place the dough on a lightly floured surface, and roll to ¼-inch thickness. Cut with a floured 4-inch snowman-shaped cookie cutter. Place the cutouts 1 inch apart on ungreased baking sheets.

3. Bake at 375°F for 7 to 9 minutes or until the edges are light golden brown. Cool on baking sheets 2 minutes. Transfer to wire racks, and cool completely (about 20 minutes).

4. Spread the white icing on the cookies. Sprinkle the white sugar on the bodies and faces of the snowmen; sprinkle black sugar on the hats. Use the green and blue icing to add scarves. Use the black decorating icing to add eyes and mouths. Use the red decorating icing to add hatbands; place 1 snowflake sprinkle on each hatband. Shape the orange fondant into 24 very small nose shapes; add 1 nose to each snowman. Add 3 cinnamon candies to each snowman for buttons. Let stand 30 minutes or until icing sets. Store between layers of waxed paper or aluminum foil.

* INGREDIENT SWAP *

Any orange gummy candy can be used instead of fondant for a snowman nose. Roll the gummy out in sugar, and cut out a small triangle with a paring knife.

GIFT TAG COOKIES

Chill baking sheets in the freezer for 15 minutes so cutouts hold their shape.

HANDS-ON TIME 35 MINUTES   TOTAL TIME 2 HOURS 10 MINUTES   MAKES 20 COOKIES

1   **(17.5-ounce) pouch sugar cookie mix**
⅓   **cup butter, softened**
1   **tablespoon all-purpose flour**
1   **large egg**
    Plastic wrap
1   **cup prepared cream cheese frosting or vanilla frosting**
    Red, green, and lime-green food coloring paste
    Ribbons

1. Stir together the first 4 ingredients until a soft dough forms. Shape into a flattened round; wrap in plastic wrap. Refrigerate 1 hour or until firm.

2. Preheat the oven to 375°F. Place the dough on a lightly floured surface, and roll to ¼-inch thickness. Cut with a floured 3-inch gift tag-shaped cookie cutter (or cut into 3- x 2-inch rectangles, and cut ½ inch diagonally off 2 corners of rectangle). Place the cutouts about 2 inches apart on ungreased baking sheets. Chill the cutouts for 15 minutes.

3. Bake at 375°F for 10 to 12 minutes or until the edges are light golden brown. Cool 2 minutes on baking sheets; transfer to wire racks, and cool completely (about 20 minutes). Use a drinking straw to make a hole at the narrow end of each gift tag cookie.

4. Place ⅓ cup frosting in each of 3 small bowls. Use food coloring to tint 1 bowl red, 1 green, and 1 lime-green. Spoon each color frosting into individual zip-top plastic freezer bags; seal bags. Snip 1 corner of each icing bag to create a small hole. Squeeze the bag to pipe details on gift tags. String the ribbon through the holes in the cookies.

THAT'S A WRAP

Wrap each cookie in a cellophane bag, and tie with a ribbon. Attach the wrapped cookie to a gift to add a sweet, personalized touch.

FESTIVE ORNAMENT COOKIES

Outline each shape before filling in with icing. This will ensure crisp icing edges.

HANDS-ON TIME 40 MINUTES   TOTAL TIME 1 HOUR 20 MINUTES   MAKES 20 COOKIES

1   (16.5-ounce) package refrigerated sugar cookie dough
¼   cup all-purpose flour
1   (7-ounce) pouch red cookie decorating icing
1   (7-ounce) pouch green cookie decorating icing
1   (7-ounce) pouch white cookie decorating icing
¼   cup red and green miniature candy-coated chocolate candies

1. Preheat the oven to 350°F. Break up the cookie dough into a medium bowl. Knead in the flour until well blended.

2. Place the dough on a lightly floured surface, and roll to ¼-inch thickness. Cut with a floured 3- to 3½-inch ornament-shaped cookie cutter. Place the cutouts 2 inches apart on ungreased baking sheets.

3. Bake at 350°F for 10 to 12 minutes or until set and the edges are lightly browned. Cool on baking sheets for 2 minutes. Transfer to wire racks, and cool completely (about 20 minutes).

4. Spread the tops of the cookies with desired-color cookie icing, and pipe preferred designs. Decorate with candies as desired.

> ✳ **INGREDIENT SWAP** ✳
> Consider substituting a package of refrigerated gingerbread cookie dough for the sugar cookie dough in this recipe.

SUGAR COOKIE STARS

Use your best-loved 3-inch holiday cutter if you don't have a star cutter on hand.

HANDS-ON TIME 1 HOUR   TOTAL TIME 2 HOURS 10 MINUTES   MAKES ABOUT 36 COOKIES

1   cup butter, softened
1   cup granulated sugar
¾   teaspoon almond extract
1   large egg
2¼   cups all-purpose flour
¼   teaspoon table salt
     White Frosting
¾   cup light blue sparkling sugar

WHITE FROSTING

MAKES 3 CUPS

1   cup butter, softened
3   cups powdered sugar, sifted
3   tablespoons heavy cream
½   teaspoon almond extract

Beat the butter and powdered sugar at low speed with an electric mixer until blended. Increase the speed to medium, and beat for 3 minutes. Add the heavy cream and almond extract, beating to the desired consistency.

1. Beat the butter and granulated sugar at medium speed with an electric mixer until light and fluffy. Add the almond extract and egg, beating until blended. Stir together the flour and salt. Gradually add to the butter mixture, beating at low speed just until blended.

2. Divide the dough into 2 equal portions; flatten each into a disk. Cover and chill for 20 minutes.

3. Preheat oven to 350°F. Place 1 portion of dough on a lightly floured surface, and roll to ⅛-inch thickness. Cut with a floured 3-inch star-shaped cookie cutter. Place the cutouts 2 inches apart on ungreased baking sheets. Repeat procedure with the remaining dough portion.

4. Bake at 350°F for 10 to 12 minutes or until the edges are lightly browned. Cool on baking sheets 5 minutes. Transfer to wire racks, and cool completely (about 20 minutes).

5. Spread White Frosting over the cookies. Sprinkle with sparkling sugar.

> ### ✳ COOKIE ROOKIE ✳
> For smooth frosting, drizzle a little in the center of the cookie, and then spread it out in an even layer using the back of a spoon or an offset spatula.

SUGAR COOKIE TREES

These 3-D cookies would be an excellent addition to the landscape of a gingerbread house.

HANDS-ON TIME 40 MINUTES   TOTAL TIME 3 HOURS 30 MINUTES   MAKES 15 ASSEMBLED COOKIES

1½ cups butter, softened
 2 cups granulated sugar
 4 large eggs
 1 teaspoon vanilla extract
 5 cups all-purpose flour
 2 teaspoons baking powder
 ½ teaspoon table salt
1½ teaspoons green gel food coloring
 1 (4⅓-ounce) tube green decorating icing
    Small yellow star sprinkles
    Green sanding sugar

1. Beat the butter at medium speed with an electric mixer until creamy. Gradually add the granulated sugar, beating well. Add the eggs and vanilla, beating well.

2. Stir together the flour, baking powder, and salt; gradually add to the butter mixture, beating at low speed just until blended. Beat in the food coloring. Cover and chill for 2 hours or until firm.

3. Preheat the oven to 375°F. Place the dough on a lightly floured surface, and roll to ¼-inch thickness. Cut with a floured 3- or 5-inch tree-shaped cutter. Place the cutouts 1 inch apart on ungreased baking sheets.

4. Bake at 375°F for 10 to 12 minutes or until set but not browned. Cool on baking sheets 2 minutes. While cookies are warm, cut half of the cookies in half vertically. Transfer to wire racks, and cool completely (about 20 minutes).

5. Use the icing to glue 2 matching cookie halves at right angles on opposite sides of center of each whole cookie. Decorate the cookies using additional icing to attach the star sprinkles and sanding sugar.

> ✳ **COOKIE ROOKIE** ✳
> Be sure to cut the trees in half while they are still warm to avoid cracks.

VANILLA-BROWN SUGAR BELLS

An offset spatula makes it easy to spread the vanilla frosting without making a mess.

HANDS-ON TIME 15 MINUTES   TOTAL TIME 1 HOUR 10 MINUTES   MAKES 30 COOKIES

Parchment paper

- 1½ cups firmly packed dark brown sugar
- 1 cup unsalted butter, softened
- 1 teaspoon vanilla bean paste or vanilla extract
- 1 large egg
- 3½ cups all-purpose flour
- 1 teaspoon baking soda
- ½ teaspoon salt
- ½ teaspoon ground cinnamon
- 1 (1-pound) container vanilla frosting

Coarse white and silver sparkling sugar, white pearl sugar, silver and white edible glitter

1. Preheat the oven to 350°F. Line baking sheets with parchment paper. Beat the brown sugar and butter at medium speed with an electric mixer until light and fluffy. Beat in the vanilla bean paste and egg. Gradually beat in the flour and next 3 ingredients on low speed.

2. Divide the dough in half. Place each half on a floured surface. Roll each half to ¼-inch thickness, using a lightly floured rolling pin. Cut the dough with a floured 3-inch bell-shaped cookie cutter. Place the cutouts, 1 inch apart, on prepared baking sheets.

3. Bake at 350°F for 10 to 12 minutes or until set. Cool 1 minute on baking sheets. Transfer to wire racks, and cool completely (about 20 minutes).

4. Microwave the frosting in a microwave-safe bowl at HIGH 30 seconds or just until pourable. Smooth the frosting over the cookies using an offset spatula. Sprinkle with assorted sugars and edible glitter. Let stand on wire racks until firm.

EASY SANTA COOKIES

Sweetened coconut flakes add an element of whimsy and texture to Santa's beard.

HANDS-ON TIME 1 HOUR   TOTAL TIME 2 HOURS   MAKES 24 COOKIES

1	(16.5-ounce) package refrigerated sugar cookie dough
¼	cup all-purpose flour
2	cups powdered sugar
2	tablespoons butter, softened
2	tablespoons milk
2	drops red liquid food coloring
¼	cup semisweet chocolate morsels
24	red cinnamon candies
⅔	cup sweetened flaked coconut
24	miniature marshmallows
	Waxed paper

1. Break up the cookie dough into a medium bowl. Knead in the flour until well blended. Shape the dough into a log. If too soft to cut into slices, chill up to 30 minutes.

2. Preheat the oven to 350°F. Cut the dough into 24 (¼-inch) slices. Place the slices 3 inches apart on ungreased baking sheets. Bake at 350°F for 8 to 12 minutes or until golden brown. Cool on baking sheets 2 minutes. Transfer to wire racks, and cool completely (about 20 minutes).

3. Stir together the powdered sugar, butter, and enough milk to make the frosting smooth and spreadable. Spoon half of the frosting into another small bowl. Add the red food coloring; stir until blended.

4. Frost each cookie with red and white frosting (see image at right). Use a small amount of frosting to attach chocolate morsels for the eyes and a cinnamon candy for the nose. Gently press coconut into the white frosting for the beard. Press 1 marshmallow into the red frosting for a tassel on the cap. Put some white frosting in a zip-top plastic freezer bag. Snip 1 corner of the bag to make a small hole. Squeeze the bag to pipe the white trim on the cap. Let stand until the frosting is set. Store between sheets of waxed paper in a tightly covered container at room temperature.

THAT'S A WRAP
Place the cookies in a paper bag, fold over the top, punch two holes, string ribbon through the holes, and tie a bow.

STAINED-GLASS ORNAMENT COOKIES

To hang these cookies, use a straw to poke a hole near the edge before baking.

HANDS-ON TIME 1 HOUR 25 MINUTES   TOTAL TIME 2 HOURS 25 MINUTES   MAKES ABOUT 36 COOKIES

Parchment paper

30 red- and green-colored hard candies

1 cup butter, softened

⅔ cup sugar

½ cup light corn syrup

2 teaspoons vanilla extract

¼ teaspoon lemon extract (optional)

3 cups all-purpose flour

¾ teaspoon baking powder

½ teaspoon table salt

White, red, and green rolled fondant

1. Preheat the oven to 350°F. Line baking sheets with parchment paper. Place each color candy in a separate zip-top plastic freezer bag; seal the bags. With a rolling pin, coarsely crush the candy; set aside.

2. Beat the butter and sugar at medium speed with an electric mixer until light and fluffy. Beat in the corn syrup, vanilla, and, if desired, lemon extract. Gradually beat in the flour, baking powder, and salt on low speed until blended.

3. Divide the dough in half. Place on a floured surface, and roll each half to ¼-inch thickness. Cut the dough with various 3-inch ornament-shaped cookie cutters. Cut out and remove several smaller dough shapes from each cookie. Place the shapes 2 inches apart on prepared baking sheets. If desired, reroll the small cutouts with the remaining dough. Fill each hole in the ornament shapes with about ½ teaspoon crushed candy.

4. Bake at 350°F for 8 to 10 minutes or until the edges are light golden brown and the candy is melted. Place baking sheets on wire racks; cool 8 minutes. Transfer to wire racks. Cool completely (about 30 minutes).

5. Roll each color fondant to ⅛-inch thickness. Using cookie cutters, cut out ornament shapes. Lightly brush the cookies with water, and press the fondant onto the surface. Cut out other shapes to decorate.

> ✳ **INGREDIENT SWAP** ✳
> Use other colored hard candies, like blues and purples, to add a variety of hues to your festive holiday ornament cookies.

CLASSIC SUGAR COOKIES

Use a toothpick to spread frosting into the crevices of these cookie canvases.

HANDS-ON TIME 1 HOUR 15 MINUTES   TOTAL TIME 2 HOURS 45 MINUTES   MAKES 24 COOKIES

1   cup butter, softened
1   cup granulated sugar
1   large egg
1   teaspoon vanilla extract
3   cups all-purpose flour
¼   teaspoon table salt
   Cooking spray
1   recipe Royal Icing (page 8)
   Green food coloring paste
24 star candy sprinkles
   Red, white, and green candies
   Red sanding sugar

1. Beat the butter at medium speed with an electric mixer 2 minutes or until creamy. Gradually add the granulated sugar, beating well. Add the egg and vanilla, beating well. Gradually add the flour and salt, beating until blended. Divide the dough in half; cover and chill 1 hour.

2. Preheat the oven to 350°F. Lightly spray baking sheets with cooking spray. Place the dough on a lightly floured surface, and roll each portion to ¼-inch thickness. Cut with desired cookie cutters. Place on prepared baking sheets 2 inches apart.

3. Bake at 350°F for 8 to 10 minutes or until the edges are lightly browned. Cool on baking sheets for 1 minute. Transfer to wire racks, and cool completely (about 20 minutes).

4. Make Royal Icing. Divide the icing and tint with food coloring. (Icing dries quickly, so keep it covered at all times. Store any leftover in an airtight container in the refrigerator, and bring to room temperature before using. Add a little water to thin it, if necessary.)

5. Spread darker green icing on bottom half of trees and lighter green icing on top halves of trees. Place a yellow star sprinkle on the top of each tree. Using icing, candies, and sanding sugar, decorate trees as desired.

> ### ✳ COOKIE ROOKIE ✳
> The amount of water you add to the icing will vary. For stiff icing, use less water. Use more water for thinner icing, perfect for piping delicate designs.

SUGAR COOKIE PRESENTS

A pair of tweezers allows for control and precision when placing decorative touches.

HANDS-ON TIME 45 MINUTES   TOTAL TIME 2 HOURS 20 MINUTES   MAKES 18 COOKIES

1 (17.5-ounce) pouch sugar cookie mix
⅓ cup butter, softened
2 tablespoons all-purpose flour
1 large egg
   Plastic wrap
1 cup ready-to-spread fluffy white frosting
¼ teaspoon green food coloring paste
4 rolls strawberry chewy fruit snack (from 5-ounce box)
2 tablespoons Wilton White nonpareil sprinkles

1. Stir together the first 4 ingredients until a dough forms. Shape the dough into a ball; flatten slightly. Wrap in plastic wrap; chill 1 hour.

2. Preheat the oven to 375°F. Unwrap dough. Place on a floured surface, and roll to ¼-inch thickness. Cut with a floured 3-inch present-shaped cookie cutter. Place the cutouts 2 inches apart on ungreased baking sheets. Bake at 375°F for 9 to 11 minutes or until lightly browned. Cool 2 minutes on baking sheets. Transfer to wire racks, and cool completely (about 20 minutes).

3. Stir together the frosting and food coloring in a small bowl until well blended. Frost the cookies. Cut and shape the fruit snacks to look like ribbons and bows; place on the cookies. Sprinkle with nonpareils. Let stand 30 minutes or until set.

REINDEER SUGAR COOKIES

You can use red decorating gel to give one of these reindeer a red nose just like Rudolph!

HANDS-ON TIME 45 MINUTES   TOTAL TIME 2 HOUR 30 MINUTES   MAKES 24 COOKIES

- 1 (6.25-ounce) pouch sugar cookie mix
- 2 tablespoons all-purpose flour
- ⅓ cup butter, melted
- 1 large egg
  Plastic wrap
- 1 (4.25-ounce) tube white decorating icing
- ½ teaspoon brown food coloring paste
- 1 cup dark chocolate frosting
  Decorating gel (optional)

1. Stir together the first 4 ingredients until a soft dough forms. Shape the dough into a ball; flatten slightly. Wrap in plastic wrap; chill 1 hour.

2. Preheat the oven to 375°F. Unwrap the dough. Place on a floured surface, and roll to ¼-inch thickness. Cut with a floured 4-inch reindeer-shaped cookie cutter. Place the cutouts 1 inch apart on ungreased baking sheets.

3. Bake at 375°F for 7 to 9 minutes or until lightly browned. Cool 1 minute on baking sheets. Transfer to wire racks, and cool completely (about 20 minutes).

4. Stir together the white icing and food coloring in a small bowl to make light brown icing. Spread the icing over the head and body of each reindeer cookie. Spoon the chocolate frosting into a zip-top plastic freezer bag. Snip 1 corner of the bag to make a small hole. Squeeze the bag to pipe the frosting on the eye, antlers, tail, and hooves of each reindeer. Use red, yellow, and green decorating gel to add a nose and collar, if desired. Let stand until set.

THAT'S A WRAP
Line a small basket with a holiday napkin, and fill it with cookies.

PEPPERMINT SHORTBREAD THINS

Peppermint glaze adds a minty-fresh zing to these crumbly shortbreads.

HANDS-ON TIME 45 MINUTES   TOTAL TIME 2 HOURS 25 MINUTES   MAKES 28 COOKIES

12	hard round peppermint candies
1	cup butter, softened
1½	cups powdered sugar
2	cups all-purpose flour
⅛	teaspoon table salt
	Plastic wrap
4	teaspoons milk
¼	teaspoon peppermint extract
¼	teaspoon red food coloring paste

1. Place the peppermint candies in a food processor. Cover; process until finely ground.

2. Beat the butter and ½ cup of the powdered sugar at medium speed with an electric mixer 3 minutes or until light and fluffy. Beat in the ground candies, flour, and salt at low speed just until blended. Shape the dough into an 8- x 2-inch log; wrap in plastic wrap. Chill 2 hours or until firm.

3. Preheat the oven to 350°F. Unwrap the dough; cut the log into ¼-inch slices. Place the slices about 2 inches apart on ungreased baking sheets.

4. Bake at 350°F for 12 to 14 minutes or until the edges are light golden brown. Cool on baking sheets 2 minutes. Transfer to wire racks, and cool completely (about 20 minutes).

5. Stir together the remaining 1 cup powdered sugar, milk, and peppermint extract in a small bowl. Divide the glaze in half. Tint half of the glaze with red food coloring. Drizzle red and white glazes over the cookies.

SNOWFLAKE SHORTBREAD

Every snowflake is unique so consider varying the decorated designs.

HANDS-ON TIME 30 MINUTES   TOTAL TIME 1 HOUR 30 MINUTES   MAKES 90 COOKIES

Parchment paper
2   cups all-purpose flour
¼   teaspoon table salt
1   cup butter, softened
1   cup powdered sugar
1   (7-ounce) pouch white
    cookie decorating icing
    Coarse white sparkling sugar
    Waxed paper

1. Preheat the oven to 325°F. Line baking sheets with parchment paper. Stir together flour and salt; set aside.

2. Beat the butter at medium speed with an electric mixer until creamy. Gradually add the powdered sugar, beating well. Gradually add the flour mixture to the butter mixture, beating at low speed just until blended.

3. Place the dough on a lightly floured surface, and roll to ⅛-inch thickness. Cut with a 2-inch snowflake-shaped cookie cutter. Place the cutouts 1 inch apart on prepared baking sheets.

4. Bake at 325°F for 11 to 13 minutes or until the edges are lightly browned. Cool on baking sheets 5 minutes. Transfer to wire racks, and cool completely (about 20 minutes). Decorate with white icing; sprinkle with sparkling sugar. Store between sheets of waxed paper in a tightly covered container at room temperature.

＊ COOKIE ROOKIE ＊

When rolling dough be sure to limit the flour on your work surface. Excess flour could affect the texture of the baked cookies.

REINDEER GINGERSNAPS

A variety of candies transform ordinary cookies into seasonal sweets.

HANDS-ON TIME 40 MINUTES   TOTAL TIME 1 HOUR 10 MINUTES   MAKES 16 COOKIES

Parchment paper
1 (14.5-ounce) package gingerbread mix
1 teaspoon meringue powder
½ teaspoon hot water
1 (12-ounce) container ready-to-spread fluffy white frosting
32 miniature candy canes
32 black licorice candies
16 sour red cherry candies

1. Preheat the oven to 375°F. Line baking sheets with parchment paper. Prepare the gingerbread dough according to the package instructions for gingersnap cookies.

2. Place the dough on a lightly floured surface, roll to ¼-inch thickness, and cut into 3½-inch ovals, using a floured egg-shaped or oval cookie cutter. Place 2 inches apart on prepared baking sheets.

3. Bake at 375°F for 8 to 10 minutes or until the edges are lightly browned. Transfer to wire racks, and cool completely (about 20 minutes).

4. Stir together the meringue powder and hot water until combined; stir in the frosting. Spoon frosting mixture into a zip-top plastic freezer bag; snip off 1 corner of the bag to make a small hole. Squeeze the bag to pipe 1 dot of frosting mixture at the top of 1 cookie; press the straight ends of 2 candy canes into the frosting to form antlers. (Prop up the candy canes as needed.) Pipe 2 large frosting ovals in the center of cookie; press 1 licorice candy in each oval to form eyes. Pipe 1 dot of frosting at bottom of cookie; press 1 cherry candy in dot to form a nose. Repeat the procedure with the remaining cookies, frosting mixture, and candies. Let stand to dry completely.

> ## ✳ COOKIE ROOKIE ✳
> Let the kids use their imaginations as they make reindeer faces on these super-cute cookies.

GINGERBREAD COOKIES

Involve the little ones by letting them decorate these spice cookies.

HANDS-ON TIME 45 MINUTES   TOTAL TIME 2 HOURS 35 MINUTES   MAKES 24 COOKIES

1   cup butter, softened
1   cup granulated sugar
1½   teaspoons baking soda
¼   cup hot water
1   cup molasses
5½   cups all-purpose flour
1½   tablespoons ground ginger
1½   teaspoons ground cinnamon
¼   teaspoon table salt
¼   teaspoon ground allspice
     Parchment paper
1   recipe Royal Icing or
     Buttermilk Frosting (page 8)
     Red and green food
     coloring (optional)
     Sugar crystals
     Snowflake sprinkles
     White and green ball candies

1. Beat the butter and granulated sugar at medium speed with a heavy-duty electric stand mixer until fluffy.

2. Stir together the baking soda and ¼ cup hot water until dissolved; stir in molasses.

3. Stir together the flour and next 4 ingredients. Add to the butter mixture alternately with molasses mixture, beginning and ending with flour mixture. Shape mixture into a ball; cover and chill 1 hour.

4. Preheat the oven to 350°F. Line baking sheets with parchment paper. Place the dough on a lightly floured surface, and roll to ¼-inch thickness. Cut the dough with a 4-inch gingerbread man-shaped cookie cutter. Place the cutouts 2 inches apart on prepared baking sheets.

5. Bake at 350°F for 15 to 18 minutes. Cool on baking sheets 2 minutes. Transfer to wire racks, and cool completely (about 30 minutes).

6. Make Royal Icing or Buttermilk Frosting. Divide the icing, and tint with food coloring, if desired. (Icing dries quickly, so keep it covered at all times.) Spoon each icing color into a small zip-top plastic freezer bag. Snip 1 corner of each bag to make a small hole. Squeeze the bag to pipe decorations on cookies. Decorate cookies as desired with sugar crystals, sprinkles, and candies. (Store any leftover icing or frosting in an airtight container in the refrigerator, and bring to room temperature before using. Add a little water to thin it if necessary.)

GINGERBREAD CHRISTMAS TREES

Work with a small bowl of warm water nearby to clean up sticky fingers.

HANDS-ON TIME 45 MINUTES   TOTAL TIME 3 HOURS 45 MINUTES   MAKES 12 COOKIES

1   (17.5-ounce) pouch gingerbread cookie mix
4   ounces butter, softened
1   teaspoon grated fresh ginger
1   large egg
1   tablespoon water
    Plastic wrap
1   (12-ounce) container ready-to-spread vanilla frosting
½   teaspoon green food coloring paste
¼   cup chocolate frosting
1   (4.25-ounce) tube white decorating icing
    Light bulb-shaped candy sprinkles
12 large yellow star-shaped candy sprinkles

1. Stir together the first 4 ingredients and 1 tablespoon water until a soft dough forms. Divide the dough in half. Wrap in plastic wrap; chill 2 hours.

2. Preheat the oven to 375°F. Unwrap the dough. Place the dough on a lightly floured surface, and roll half of dough to ¼-inch thickness. Cut with a floured 5-inch Christmas tree-shaped cookie cutter. Place the cutouts 2 inches apart on ungreased baking sheets. Repeat with remaining half of dough. Bake at 375°F for 8 to 10 minutes or until the edges are set. Cool 2 minutes on baking sheets. Transfer to wire racks, and cool completely (about 20 minutes).

3. Stir together the vanilla frosting and green food coloring until blended. Spread on the cookies. Spread the chocolate frosting on the base of each cookie for the tree stump. With the white icing, starting at top, pipe thin, swooping lines to look like light strands. Decorate with light bulb candy sprinkles. Place a yellow star sprinkle at the top of each cookie. Let stand 30 minutes or until set.

SNOWCAPPED PEANUT BUTTER TREES

Reusable pastry bags might seem cost effective, but stick to disposable if you're a beginner.

HANDS-ON TIME 40 MINUTES   TOTAL TIME 1 HOUR 5 MINUTES   MAKES 18 COOKIES

1   (16.5-ounce) package refrigerated peanut butter cookie dough
¼   cup all-purpose flour
¾   cup chopped chocolate-covered peanut butter cup candies
¾   cup chocolate creamy ready-to-spread frosting
½   cup fluffy white whipped ready-to-spread frosting
½   teaspoon green food coloring paste
1   tablespoon small white candy sprinkles
1   tablespoon white snowflake sprinkles

1. Preheat the oven to 350°F. Break up the cookie dough into a medium bowl. Knead in the flour until well blended. Stir in the peanut butter cup candies.

2. Place the dough on a lightly floured surface, and roll to ¼-inch thickness. Cut with a 4-inch Christmas tree-shaped cookie cutter. Place 2 inches apart on ungreased baking sheets.

3. Bake at 350°F for 8 to 10 minutes or until set and the edges are lightly browned. Cool on baking sheets 2 minutes. Transfer to wire racks, and cool completely (about 20 minutes).

4. Spread a thin layer of chocolate frosting on each cookie. Stir together the white frosting and green food coloring. Spoon the green frosting into a decorating bag fitted with a small plain tip. Pipe green frosting onto the cookies. Decorate with white candy and snowflake sprinkles.

NOTE: We tested with Reese's Peanut Butter Cups.

ORANGE-FROSTED CORNMEAL STARS

Cornmeal batter adds a complex crunch to traditional sugar cookies.

HANDS-ON TIME 35 MINUTES   TOTAL TIME 2 HOURS 15 MINUTES   MAKES 20 COOKIES

1	cup butter, softened
1	cup granulated sugar
2	large egg whites
1	large egg yolk
2	tablespoons grated orange rind
5	tablespoons fresh orange juice
1½	teaspoons vanilla extract
2¾	cups all-purpose flour
⅔	cup yellow cornmeal
1½	teaspoons baking powder
½	teaspoon table salt
	Plastic wrap
	Parchment paper
2	cups powdered sugar

1. Beat the butter and granulated sugar at medium speed with an electric mixer until light and fluffy. Beat the egg whites at high speed in a separate bowl until stiff peaks form; add to the butter mixture, beating just until blended. Add the egg yolk, 1½ tablespoons of the orange rind, 2 tablespoons of the orange juice, and vanilla, beating just until blended.

2. Stir together the flour and next 3 ingredients; gradually add to the butter mixture, beating just until blended after each addition.

3. Shape the dough into a ball, and divide in half. Flatten each half into a 5-inch disk; wrap each disk in plastic wrap. Freeze the dough 30 minutes.

4. Preheat the oven to 350°F. Line baking sheets with parchment paper. Place the dough on a floured surface, and roll the dough, 1 portion at a time, to ¼-inch thickness. Cut with a floured 4- or 5-inch star-shaped cookie cutter. Reroll the trimmings to make additional cookies. Place the cutouts, 1 inch apart, on prepared baking sheets.

5. Bake at 350°F for 14 minutes or until golden. Cool 5 minutes on baking sheets. Transfer to wire racks, and cool completely (about 20 minutes).

6. Stir together the powdered sugar, the remaining ½ tablespoon orange rind, and the remaining 3 tablespoons orange juice in a medium bowl, stirring with a whisk until smooth. Spread the frosting on the stars. Place the cookies on wire racks, and let stand for 30 minutes until the frosting is set.

CHRISTMAS CLASSICS

Gather around the tree on Christmas day, and share these tried-and-true baked treats with your friends and family.

PECAN LINZER COOKIES

For different flavors and colors, use an assortment of jams to fill the centers of these beauties.

HANDS-ON TIME 1 HOUR   TOTAL TIME 6 HOURS 10 MINUTES   MAKES 24 SANDWICH COOKIES

2¼ cups all-purpose flour
1   cup pecan halves
1   teaspoon ground cinnamon
½   teaspoon ground cloves
1   cup butter, softened
⅓   cup granulated sugar
1   teaspoon grated lemon rind
1   large egg
1   large egg yolk
    Plastic wrap
    Parchment paper
¼   cup powdered sugar
6   teaspoons peach jam
    (or other desired flavors)

1. Pulse the first 4 ingredients in a food processor until finely ground.

2. Beat the butter, granulated sugar, and rind at medium speed with an electric mixer 1 minute. Add the egg and egg yolk; beat 30 seconds. Scrape the bowl; beat 30 seconds. Add the flour mixture, beating until combined.

3. Shape the dough into 2 (½-inch-thick) rectangles. Wrap each rectangle in plastic wrap, and chill 4 hours to 3 days.

4. Generously flour both sides of the dough; place on parchment paper. Roll each into a 14- x 10-inch rectangle. Cut each rectangle into 24 (2-inch) squares, rerolling the scraps as needed. Chill on the parchment paper 30 minutes.

5. Preheat the oven to 350°F. Line baking sheets with parchment paper. Place the cookies 1 inch apart on prepared baking sheets. Cut the centers out of half of the cookies with a lightly floured 1¼-inch square cutter. (If desired, place dough centers on a parchment paper–lined baking sheet; chill 15 minutes, and bake as directed.)

6. Bake at 350°F for 12 to 14 minutes or until the edges are golden. Cool completely on parchment paper on a wire rack (about 20 minutes).

7. Sprinkle powdered sugar over cutout cookies. Spread about ¼ teaspoon jam onto each solid cookie; top with cutout cookies.

THAT'S A WRAP
Stack cookies on a pretty tray from a flea market, wrap with cellophane, and tie with ribbon.

PLUM-CARDAMOM LINZER COOKIES

Cardamom, which is similar to ginger, adds a savory note to these jam-filled cookies.

HANDS-ON TIME 50 MINUTES   TOTAL TIME 2 HOURS 10 MINUTES   MAKES 12 SANDWICH COOKIES

¾   cup slivered almonds, toasted and ground
2½   cups all-purpose flour
1   teaspoon grated lemon rind
½   teaspoon baking powder
½   teaspoon ground cardamom
¼   teaspoon table salt
1¼   cups butter, softened
1   cup powdered sugar, sifted
    Plastic wrap
    Parchment paper
1   cup plum jam or jelly
3   tablespoons powdered sugar

1. Stir together the first 6 ingredients with a whisk. Beat the butter in a large bowl at medium speed with an electric mixer until creamy. Gradually add 1 cup powdered sugar; beat until light and fluffy. Beat in the flour mixture at low speed just until blended. Divide the dough in half. Cover with plastic wrap; chill 1 hour or until firm.

2. Preheat oven to 350°F. Line baking sheets with parchment paper.

3. Place the dough on a lightly floured surface, and roll each portion of the dough to ⅛-inch thickness. Cut with a floured 2½-inch fluted round or scalloped cookie cutter. Cut the centers out of half of the cookies with a floured 1¼-inch fluted round cookie cutter. Place the solid cookies, cutout cookies, and cutout centers, 1 inch apart, on prepared baking sheets.

4. Bake at 350°F for 9 to 11 minutes or until the edges are light golden. Transfer to wire racks, and cool completely (about 20 minutes). Spread each solid cookie with 2 teaspoons jam. Sift 3 tablespoons powdered sugar over cutout cookies and cutout centers. Top each solid cookie with a cutout cookie. Spoon additional jam into the opening of each cutout cookie, if desired.

THAT'S A WRAP
The center cutouts are still delicious! Package linzer cookies in a unique container with the centers as an extra treat.

CHRISTMAS LINZER COOKIES

Raspberry jam is the traditional filling for linzer cookies.

HANDS-ON TIME 50 MINUTES   TOTAL TIME 2 HOURS 20 MINUTES   MAKES 24 SANDWICH COOKIES

1¼ cups butter, softened
1 cup powdered sugar
¾ cup slivered almonds, toasted and ground
2½ cups all-purpose flour
1 teaspoon grated lemon rind
½ teaspoon baking powder
¼ teaspoon table salt
Parchment paper
½ cup strawberry or raspberry jam
2 tablespoons powdered sugar

1. Beat the butter at medium speed with an electric mixer until creamy; gradually add 1 cup powdered sugar, beating until light and fluffy. Stir together the ground almonds, flour, and next 3 ingredients in a medium bowl. Beat the flour mixture into the butter mixture at low speed just until blended. Divide the dough in half. Cover; chill 1 hour or until firm.

2. Preheat the oven to 350°F. Line baking sheets with parchment paper. Place the dough on a lightly floured surface, and roll each portion of dough to ⅛-inch thickness. Cut with a floured 2½-inch round or fluted cookie cutter, rerolling the dough once. Using a 1-inch Christmas tree–shaped cookie cutter (or other desired shape), cut out centers of half of the cookies. Place the solid cookies, cutout cookies, and cutout centers 1 inch apart on prepared baking sheets.

3. Bake at 350°F for 10 to 12 minutes or until the edges are light golden brown. Immediately transfer to wire racks, and cool completely (about 20 minutes). Spread each solid cookie with 1 teaspoon jam. Sprinkle 2 tablespoons powdered sugar over the cutout cookies and cutout centers. Top each solid cookie with a cutout cookie. Store loosely covered.

PISTACHIO THUMBPRINT COOKIES

Flecked with green pistachios and filled with red jam, these thumbprints are very festive.

HANDS-ON TIME 25 MINUTES   TOTAL TIME 40 MINUTES   MAKES ABOUT 33 COOKIES

¾   cup pistachios
1   cup butter, softened
½   cup sugar
2   large egg yolks
1   teaspoon vanilla extract
½   teaspoon almond extract
2   cups all-purpose flour
⅓   cup seedless raspberry jam

1. Preheat the oven to 350°F. Pulse the pistachios in a food processor 10 or 12 times or until the pistachios are chopped.

2. Beat the butter at medium speed with an electric mixer about 2 to 3 minutes or until creamy. Gradually add the sugar, beating well. Add the egg yolks and extracts, beating well. Gradually add the flour, beating at low speed just until blended. Stir in chopped pistachios.

3. Shape the dough into 33 (1-inch) balls; place 2 inches apart on ungreased baking sheets. Press a thumb or the end of a wooden spoon handle into the center of each ball, forming an indentation. Spoon about ½ teaspoon jam into each indentation.

4. Bake at 350°F for 12 to 15 minutes or until the edges are golden brown. Cool on baking sheets 5 minutes. Transfer to wire racks, and cool completely (about 20 minutes).

＊ INGREDIENT SWAP ＊

Fill the center with your favorite jam. Our jam of choice is raspberry, but strawberry or apricot would be delicious, too.

CHOCOLATE-PEANUT BUTTER THUMBPRINT COOKIES

Chocolate and peanut butter, a classic pairing, collide in these thumbprint cookies.

HANDS-ON TIME 45 MINUTES   TOTAL TIME 1 HOUR 10 MINUTES   MAKES 20 COOKIES

1   (16.5-ounce) package refrigerated chocolate chip cookie dough
¼   cup all-purpose flour
½   cup peanut butter morsels
½   cup dry-roasted peanuts, finely chopped
1   cup chocolate creamy ready-to-spread frosting
20   miniature chocolate-covered peanut butter cup candies

1. Preheat the oven to 350°F. Break up the cookie dough into a large bowl. Knead in the flour and peanut butter morsels until well blended.

2. Shape the dough into 20 (1-inch) balls; roll balls in chopped peanuts to coat completely, pressing gently. Place the balls 2 inches apart on ungreased baking sheets. Press a thumb or the end of a wooden spoon handle into the center of each ball, forming an indentation, but do not press through to the baking sheet.

3. Bake at 350°F for 15 to 18 minutes or until the edges are set. Cool on baking sheets 5 minutes. Remake the indentations. Transfer to wire racks, and cool completely (about 20 minutes).

4. Place the frosting in a small zip-top plastic freezer bag. Snip off 1 corner of the bag to make a small hole. Squeeze about 2 teaspoons frosting in the center of each cookie to fill the indentation. Place 1 peanut butter cup candy in the middle of the frosting-filled center.

NOTE: We tested with Reese's Peanut Butter Cups.

❊ INGREDIENT SWAP ❊
Consider using different bite-size candy bars instead of the chocolate-covered peanut butter cup candies.

WALNUT-TOPPED GINGER DROP COOKIES

Enjoy these nutty ginger cookies at a celebration—they bring out the holiday cheer.

HANDS-ON TIME 1 HOUR   TOTAL TIME 1 HOUR   MAKES 42 COOKIES

½ cup packed brown sugar
½ cup butter, softened
1 teaspoon vanilla extract
1 large egg
2 cups all-purpose flour
¼ cup half-and-half
3 tablespoons finely chopped crystallized ginger
½ teaspoon baking soda
½ teaspoon table salt
½ teaspoon ground cardamom
42 walnut halves
3 tablespoons white vanilla morsels

1. Preheat the oven to 375°F. Beat the brown sugar and butter at medium speed with an electric mixer until light and fluffy. Beat in the vanilla and egg. Beat in the remaining ingredients except the walnuts and white vanilla morsels at low speed until well blended.

2. Drop the dough by rounded tablespoonfuls 2 inches apart onto ungreased baking sheets. Press 1 walnut half onto each cookie.

3. Bake at 375°F for 6 to 9 minutes or until the edges are set and light golden brown. Immediately transfer to wire racks, and cool completely (about 20 minutes).

4. Place the white vanilla morsels in a small zip-top plastic freezer bag; seal the bag. Microwave at HIGH 30 to 45 seconds or until softened. Squeeze the bag until morsels are smooth. Snip off 1 corner of the bag to make a small hole; squeeze the bag to drizzle melted morsels over the cookies.

MAPLE-PRALINE COOKIES

Praline sweetness and drop-cookie softness combine in these flavorful treats.

HANDS-ON TIME 30 MINUTES   TOTAL TIME 2 HOURS 22 MINUTES   MAKES 48 COOKIES

¾   cup butter, softened
¼   cup shortening
1   cup packed brown sugar
1   tablespoon maple syrup
1   large egg
2   cups all-purpose flour
½   teaspoon baking soda
¼   teaspoon table salt
     Maple-Praline Frosting
48   pecan halves, lightly toasted

MAPLE-PRALINE FROSTING

MAKES 1 CUP

1   cup firmly packed light brown sugar
⅓   cup whipping cream
2   tablespoons maple syrup
1   cup powdered sugar

Combine the brown sugar and whipping cream in a 2-quart saucepan. Cook over medium heat, stirring constantly, until the mixture comes to a boil; boil 4 minutes. (Do not stir.) Remove from heat; stir in the maple syrup. Gradually stir in the powdered sugar until smooth. Use immediately.

1. Beat the butter and shortening at medium speed with an electric mixer until creamy; gradually add the sugar, beating until light and fluffy. Add the maple syrup and egg, beating until blended.

2. Stir together the flour, baking soda, and salt; gradually add to the butter mixture, beating until blended. Cover and chill the dough 1 hour.

3. Preheat the oven to 350°F. Drop the dough by rounded tablespoonfuls onto ungreased baking sheets.

4. Bake at 350°F for 9 to 10 minutes or until the edges are lightly browned. Cool on baking sheets 1 minute. Transfer to wire racks, and cool completely (about 20 minutes).

5. Spread Maple-Praline Frosting over the cookies. Top each cookie with 1 pecan half.

✳ COOKIE ROOKIE ✳

When using brown sugar in baking, it's important to firmly pack the measuring cup for best results.

MINTY DELIGHT CANDY COOKIES

A dash of crème de menthe intensifies the flavor of the peppermint candy pairing.

HANDS-ON TIME 30 MINUTES   TOTAL TIME 1 HOUR 5 MINUTES   MAKES 18 COOKIES

Parchment paper
1   (16.5-ounce) package refrigerated chocolate chip cookie dough
½   cup thin rectangular crème de menthe chocolate candies, unwrapped, chopped
18 small round chocolate-covered creamy mints
1   cup powdered sugar
2   tablespoons unsweetened baking cocoa
2   tablespoons crème de menthe
½   teaspoon vanilla extract
1½ teaspoons water

1. Preheat the oven to 350°F. Line baking sheets with parchment paper. Break up the cookie dough and ¼ cup of the chopped mint candies in a large bowl. Knead with hands until well mixed. Scoop the dough by rounded tablespoonfuls. Press 1 chocolate-covered mint into the center, and roll into a ball to cover the mint. Repeat to make 18 balls. Place the balls 2½ inches apart on prepared baking sheets.

2. Bake at 350°F for 10 to 12 minutes or until the edges are set. Cool on baking sheet 5 minutes. Transfer to wire racks, and cool completely (about 20 minutes).

3. Combine the powdered sugar, cocoa, crème de menthe, vanilla, and 1½ teaspoons water in a small bowl, stirring until smooth. Spread about 2 teaspoons of the glaze in the center of each cookie. Sprinkle the remaining ¼ cup chopped mint candies evenly over the glazed cookies.

CHOCOLATE-DIPPED ORANGE COOKIES

Grated orange rind paired with flaked coconut boosts the tropical flavor.

HANDS-ON TIME 20 MINUTES   TOTAL TIME 2 HOURS 40 MINUTES   MAKES 48 COOKIES

1 cup butter, softened
½ cup powdered sugar
1 teaspoon grated orange rind
1 teaspoon orange extract
2 cups all-purpose flour
1 cup semisweet chocolate morsels
¾ cup sweetened flaked coconut, lightly toasted
Additional grated orange rind (optional)

1. Beat the butter in a large bowl at medium speed with an electric mixer until creamy. Gradually add the powdered sugar, beating well. Stir in 1 teaspoon orange rind and orange extract. Gradually add the flour, beating well. Cover; chill 1 hour.

2. Preheat the oven to 350°F. Divide the dough in half. Return 1 portion to refrigerator. Divide the remaining portion into 24 pieces. Shape each piece into a 2½- x ½-inch log on a lightly floured surface. Place the logs about 2 inches apart on ungreased baking sheets. Repeat with the remaining dough.

3. Bake at 350°F for 12 minutes or until lightly golden. Cool on baking sheets 3 minutes. Transfer to wire racks, and cool completely (about 20 minutes).

4. Microwave the chocolate morsels in a small microwave-safe bowl, uncovered, at HIGH 1 minute to 1 minute 30 seconds, stirring once, until softened and morsels can be stirred smooth. Dip one tip of each cookie in the melted chocolate, and sprinkle with coconut and, if desired, orange rind. Return to wire racks; let stand until set (about 30 minutes).

PEPPERMINT MERINGUE COOKIES

To enhance the swirl design, use a food-safe paintbrush inside the piping bag.

HANDS-ON TIME 30 MINUTES   TOTAL TIME 5 HOURS 30 MINUTES   MAKES 90 COOKIES

Parchment paper
6   large egg whites
1½   teaspoons white vinegar
1½   cups sugar
1   teaspoon peppermint extract
Red food coloring gel

CHOCOLATE-DIPPED PEPPERMINT MERINGUE COOKIES

Prepare the recipe as directed. Melt 2 cups milk chocolate morsels in the microwave on HIGH for 30 seconds to 1 minute, stirring after 30 seconds, until melted and smooth. Dip the bottom of each cooled cookie in melted chocolate, and place on a parchment paper–lined baking sheet. Let stand 15 minutes or until the chocolate sets.

1. Preheat the oven to 200°F. Line baking sheets with parchment paper. Let the egg whites stand at room temperature 20 minutes. Beat the egg whites at high speed with an electric mixer, using the whisk attachment, until stiff peaks form. Reduce the speed to medium. Add the vinegar; add the sugar, ½ cup at a time, and beat until blended. Beat 2 minutes. Add the extract, beating until blended.

2. Paint 3 or 4 evenly spaced thin stripes of red food coloring gel on the inside of a pastry bag, starting at the tip and ending three-fourths of the way up the bag. Gently spoon the meringue into the center of the bag, filling three-fourths full. Snip end of bag. Pipe the meringue by 2 tablespoonfuls onto prepared baking sheets, leaving 1 inch between each cookie. Repeat with the remaining meringue, using a clean pastry bag for each batch.

3. Bake at 200°F for 2 hours. Turn off the oven, and let the meringues stand in the oven until completely cool (about 3 hours).

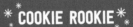

✳ COOKIE ROOKIE ✳
Chilled eggs separate easiest. Leave eggs in the fridge until you need to use them.

CHOCOLATE-DIPPED PECAN SHORTBREAD SQUARES

For the best-tasting results, use high-quality semisweet baking chocolate.

HANDS-ON TIME 40 MINUTES   TOTAL TIME 3 HOURS 55 MINUTES   MAKES 48 SQUARES

1   cup pecan halves
1   cup butter, softened
¾   cup sugar
1   teaspoon vanilla extract
2   cups all-purpose flour
¼   teaspoon table salt
    Plastic wrap
    Parchment paper
2   (4-ounce) semisweet
    chocolate baking bars,
    chopped
    Finely chopped pecans

1. Preheat the oven to 350°F. Bake the pecan halves in a single layer in a shallow pan for 8 to 10 minutes or until toasted and fragrant, stirring halfway through. Cool completely. Finely chop pecans.

2. Beat the butter at medium speed with an electric mixer until creamy; gradually add the sugar, beating until well blended. Add the vanilla; beat until blended. Stir together the flour and salt; gradually add to the butter mixture, beating at low speed just until blended. Stir in the toasted pecans.

3. Divide the dough into 2 equal portions; shape each portion into a 6- x 2-inch square log. Wrap tightly in plastic wrap, and chill 2 hours.

4. Preheat the oven to 350°F. Cut the logs into ¼-inch slices. Place 1 inch apart on ungreased baking sheets. Bake at 350°F for 14 to 16 minutes or until edges are golden brown. Cool on baking sheets 5 minutes. Transfer to wire racks, and cool completely (about 20 minutes). Line baking sheets with parchment paper.

5. Microwave the chocolate in a microwave-safe bowl at HIGH 1 to 1½ minutes or until melted and smooth, stirring at 30-second intervals. Dip each cookie halfway into the melted chocolate, letting the excess drip off. Place on prepared baking sheets. Sprinkle with chopped pecans. Let stand 30 minutes or until set.

✳ COOKIE ROOKIE ✳

Speed along this recipe by freezing the dough logs for 1 hour instead of chilling them for 2 hours in the refrigerator.

EGGNOG
CRACKLE
COOKIES

EGGNOG CRACKLE COOKIES

Finish these rich rum-infused cookies with powdered sugar.

HANDS-ON TIME 25 MINUTES   TOTAL TIME 1 HOUR 30 MINUTES   MAKES 42 COOKIES

Parchment paper
1 (15.25-ounce) box French vanilla cake mix with pudding
1 large egg, slightly beaten
1 (8-ounce) container frozen whipped topping, thawed
1 teaspoon ground nutmeg
½ teaspoon rum extract
1 cup powdered sugar
Waxed paper

1. Preheat the oven to 350°F. Line baking sheets with parchment paper.

2. Stir together cake mix, egg, whipped topping, ½ teaspoon of the nutmeg, and extract with a wooden spoon until smooth. Stir together the powdered sugar and the remaining ½ teaspoon nutmeg in a small bowl. Drop the batter by tablespoonfuls into the powdered sugar mixture; roll to coat. Place the cookies, 2 inches apart, onto prepared baking sheets.

3. Bake at 350°F for 13 to 15 minutes or until the edges are light golden brown. Cool 5 minutes on baking sheets. Transfer to wire racks. Sprinkle the warm cookies with the remaining powdered sugar mixture. Cool completely (about 20 minutes). Store cooled cookies tightly covered between sheets of waxed paper.

SPICED ALMOND-CHOCOLATE CRINKLES

These spicy, chocolaty bites bring melt-in-your-mouth goodness to all.

HANDS-ON TIME 1 HOUR 30 MINUTES   TOTAL TIME 2 HOURS 30 MINUTES   MAKES 60 COOKIES

¼ cup butter

4 ounces unsweetened baking chocolate, chopped

4 large eggs

2 cups all-purpose flour

2 cups granulated sugar

½ cup chopped almonds

2 teaspoons baking powder

½ teaspoon table salt

½ teaspoon ground ginger

½ teaspoon ground cinnamon

¼ teaspoon ground cloves

   Plastic wrap

¾ cup powdered sugar

   Cooking spray

1. Melt the butter and chocolate in a 3-quart saucepan over low until smooth, stirring constantly. Remove from heat, and cool slightly, (about 5 minutes).

2. Add the eggs to the chocolate mixture, beating with a spoon until well blended. Add the flour and the next 7 ingredients, stirring until well blended. Cover the dough with plastic wrap; chill at least 1 hour for easier handling.

3. Preheat the oven to 300°F. Place the powdered sugar in a small bowl. Shape the dough into 1-inch balls; roll in the powdered sugar, coating heavily. Place the balls 2 inches apart on baking sheets coated with cooking spray.

4. Bake at 300°F for 13 to 18 minutes or until set. Immediately transfer to wire racks, and cool completely (about 20 minutes).

✳ COOKIE ROOKIE ✳
Make sure your holiday spices are still fresh before you start baking with them. Keep them in a cool dry place, and date them to ensure the best flavor.

MOLASSES CRISPS

Flavors of cinnamon and sweet molasses permeate this crisp holiday cookie.

HANDS-ON TIME 24 MINUTES   TOTAL TIME 1 HOUR 12 MINUTES   MAKES ABOUT 36 COOKIES

½ cup butter, softened
¼ cup shortening
1 cup granulated sugar
¼ cup molasses
3 tablespoons minced crystallized ginger
1 large egg
1¾ cups all-purpose flour
1 teaspoon baking soda
1 teaspoon ground cinnamon
¼ teaspoon ground cloves
¾ cup turbinado sugar

1. Preheat the oven to 350°F. Beat the butter, shortening, and granulated sugar at medium speed with an electric mixer until light and fluffy. Add the molasses, crystallized ginger, and egg, beating just until blended.

2. Stir together the flour and next 3 ingredients in a small bowl; gradually add to the butter mixture, beating at low speed just until blended.

3. Place the turbinado sugar in a bowl. Shape the dough into 1-inch balls; roll the balls in turbinado sugar. Place 3 inches apart on ungreased baking sheets.

4. Bake at 350°F for 12 to 14 minutes or until browned and crisp. Transfer to wire racks, and cool completely (about 20 minutes).

THAT'S A WRAP

Mismatched glasses double as packages for stacks of cookie crisps. Tie on a festive ornament for a perfect presentation.

CHOCOLATE-PEPPERMINT SANDWICHES

These chocolate and peppermint handheld treats are the best holiday combination.

HANDS-ON TIME 45 MINUTES   TOTAL TIME 4 HOURS 15 MINUTES   MAKES 32 SANDWICH COOKIES

2 cups all-purpose flour

⅓ cup unsweetened dark cocoa

½ teaspoon baking powder

¼ teaspoon table salt

1⅓ cups butter, softened

1 cup granulated sugar

1 large egg

1 teaspoon peppermint extract

Plastic wrap

Cooking spray

4 ounces cream cheese, softened

2½ cups powdered sugar

15 hard round peppermint candies, crushed

1. Stir together the flour, cocoa, baking powder, and salt.

2. Beat 1 cup of the butter and the granulated sugar at medium speed with an electric mixer until creamy. Add the egg and peppermint extract; beat until well blended. Gradually beat in the flour mixture. Divide the dough in half. Shape each half into a 13- x 1½-inch log. Wrap tightly in plastic wrap; freeze 2 hours.

3. Preheat the oven to 325°F. Cut each log into 32 (about ¼-inch) slices. Place the slices 1 inch apart on baking sheets coated with cooking spray. Bake at 325°F for 12 to 13 minutes or until set. Cool on baking sheets 2 minutes. Transfer to wire racks, and cool completely (about 20 minutes).

4. Beat the remaining ⅓ cup butter and cream cheese at medium speed with an electric mixer until creamy. Gradually beat in the powdered sugar until smooth.

5. For each sandwich cookie, spread about 2 teaspoons filling on the bottom of 1 cookie. Top with a second cookie, bottom side down; gently press together. Place the crushed candies in a bowl. Roll sides of the sandwich cookies in the crushed candies.

CANDY CANE BISCOTTI

Place the cookies on a wire rack over waxed paper to catch any drips as you drizzle.

HANDS-ON TIME 14 MINUTES   TOTAL TIME 2 HOURS 30 MINUTES   MAKES ABOUT 30 BISCOTTI

¾ cup granulated sugar
½ cup butter, softened
2 large eggs, lightly beaten
2½ cups all-purpose flour
2 teaspoons baking powder
¼ teaspoon table salt
1 tablespoon peppermint schnapps
1 teaspoon vanilla extract
¾ cup crushed soft peppermint sticks
   Waxed paper
1 (4-ounce) dark chocolate baking bar, chopped
   Coarse sparkling sugar

1. Preheat the oven to 350°F. Beat the sugar and butter at medium speed with an electric mixer until creamy. Add the eggs, 1 at a time, beating until blended after each addition. Stir together the flour, baking powder, and salt; gradually add to the butter mixture, beating until blended. Stir in peppermint schnapps and vanilla. Stir in ½ cup of the crushed peppermint.

2. Divide the dough in half. Shape each portion of dough into a 9- x 2-inch log on a lightly greased baking sheet, using lightly floured hands.

3. Bake at 350°F for 28 to 30 minutes or until firm. Transfer to wire racks; cool completely (about 1 hour). Cut each log diagonally into ½-inch slices with a serrated knife, using a gentle sawing motion. Place the slices, cut sides up, on baking sheets.

4. Bake at 350°F for 10 minutes; turn the cookies over, and bake 8 more minutes. Transfer to wire racks set over waxed paper, and cool completely (about 30 minutes).

5. Microwave the chocolate in a small microwave-safe bowl at HIGH 30 to 60 seconds or until melted and smooth, stirring at 30-second intervals. Drizzle the chocolate over the tops of the biscotti; sprinkle with coarse sugar and the remaining ¼ cup crushed peppermint. Let stand 30 minutes or until the chocolate is set.

* INGREDIENT SWAP *

You also may drizzle these cookies with milk chocolate or white chocolate, whichever you prefer.

CHOCOLATE-CRANBERRY BISCOTTI

If you prefer, substitute dried cherries for the cranberries for year-round enjoyment.

HANDS-ON TIME 15 MINUTES   TOTAL TIME 2 HOURS 20 MINUTES   MAKES 24 BISCOTTI

1   (16.5-ounce) package refrigerated chocolate chip cookie dough
⅓   cup unsweetened baking cocoa
½   teaspoon almond extract
½   cup sweetened dried cranberries
½   cup sliced almonds, toasted
    Parchment paper
4   ounces semisweet baking chocolate, chopped

1. Preheat the oven to 350°F.

2. Break up the cookie dough into a large bowl. Stir in the cocoa and almond extract until well blended. Stir in the cranberries and almonds. Divide the dough in half.

3. Line a baking sheet with parchment paper. Shape each dough half into a 10- x 2-inch rectangle on parchment paper, about ¾-inch thick and 4 inches apart.

4. Bake at 350°F for 25 to 30 minutes or until the center is firm to the touch. Cool 15 minutes. Carefully cut the baked rectangles diagonally into ½-inch slices using a serrated knife. Place the slices, cut sides down, on the same baking sheet.

5. Bake at 350°F for 8 minutes. Carefully turn the slices over; bake 8 more minutes or until crisp. Cool completely on baking sheet (about 20 minutes).

6. Microwave the semisweet chocolate in a small microwave-safe bowl at HIGH 1 minute, stirring after 30 seconds, until softened and the chocolate can be stirred smooth. Spoon the chocolate into a zip-top plastic freezer bag. Snip off 1 corner of the bag to make a small hole; squeeze the bag to drizzle melted chocolate over the cookies. Chill 30 minutes or until set.

HAZELNUT AND BROWN BUTTER BISCOTTI

Personalize the biscotti with powdered sugar, a chocolate drizzle, or both.

HANDS-ON TIME 22 MINUTES   TOTAL TIME 2 HOURS 15 MINUTES   MAKES 24 BISCOTTI

Cooking spray
½   cup butter
1   cup granulated sugar
2   large eggs
2   tablespoons hazelnut liqueur
2½   cups all-purpose flour
1½   teaspoons baking powder
¼   teaspoon table salt
1½   cups blanched hazelnuts,
     chopped and toasted

1. Preheat the oven to 350°F. Lightly coat a baking sheet with cooking spray. Cook the butter in a 2-quart heavy saucepan over medium, stirring constantly, 6 to 8 minutes or just until the butter begins to turn golden brown. Immediately remove pan from heat, and pour the butter into a medium bowl. (Butter will continue to darken if left in the saucepan.) Let stand 20 minutes or until room temperature.

2. Beat the cooled butter, granulated sugar, eggs, and liqueur at medium speed with an electric mixer until creamy.

3. Stir together the flour, baking powder, and salt; add to the butter mixture, beating at low speed just until blended. Stir in the hazelnuts.

4. Divide the dough in half. Lightly flour hands, and shape each portion into a 9- x 2-inch slightly flattened log on the baking sheet.

5. Bake at 350°F for 30 minutes or until golden brown. Cool on baking sheet 5 minutes. Transfer to a wire rack, and cool completely (about 1 hour).

6. Cut each log diagonally into ¾-inch slices with a serrated knife, using a gentle sawing motion; place the slices on ungreased baking sheets.

7. Bake at 350°F for 8 minutes; turn the cookies over, and bake 15 to 20 more minutes. Transfer to wire racks, and cool completely (about 30 minutes).

CHERRY-CHOCOLATE ICEBOX COOKIES

Ribbon scraps from previous crafting projects add a pretty element to homemade gifts.

HANDS-ON TIME 18 MINUTES   TOTAL TIME 2 HOURS 42 MINUTES   MAKES ABOUT 42 COOKIES

2⅔ cups all-purpose flour
⅓ cup unsweetened cocoa
½ teaspoon baking powder
¼ teaspoon table salt
1 cup butter, softened
1 cup sugar
1 large egg
1 tablespoon cherry liqueur
¾ cup dried cherries, chopped
1 (4-ounce) semisweet chocolate baking bar, chopped
   Waxed paper
   Plastic wrap

1. Stir together the first 4 ingredients. Beat the butter and sugar at medium speed with an electric mixer until light and fluffy. Add the egg and liqueur, beating just until blended. Gradually add the flour mixture, beating just until blended after each addition. Stir in the cherries and chocolate.

2. Shape the dough into 2 (10-inch) logs using waxed paper. Wrap tightly in plastic wrap, and chill at least 2 hours.

3. Preheat the oven to 350°F. Cut logs into ½-inch slices. Place 1 inch apart on ungreased baking sheets. Bake at 350°F for 12 minutes or until set. Transfer to wire racks, and cool completely (about 20 minutes).

> ## ✳ INGREDIENT SWAP ✳
> You can substitute 1½ teaspoons vanilla extract for the cherry liqueur.

CINNAMON CHIP ICEBOX COOKIES

Other flavored baking chips, like chocolate, would taste divine with the toasted pecans.

HANDS-ON TIME 1 HOUR   TOTAL TIME 9 HOURS   MAKES 72 COOKIES

1 cup butter, softened
2 cups sugar
2 large eggs
2 teaspoons vanilla extract
4 cups all-purpose flour
1 (10-ounce) package cinnamon-flavored baking chips
1 cup chopped pecans, toasted
Waxed paper

1. Beat the butter at medium speed with an electric mixer until creamy. Gradually add the sugar, beating well. Add the eggs and vanilla, beating until blended. Gradually add the flour, beating at low speed just until blended. Stir in the baking chips and pecans.

2. Divide the dough into 3 (2-cup) portions; roll each portion into a 12-inch log. Wrap the logs in waxed paper. Chill 8 hours, or freeze in an airtight container up to 3 months.

3. Preheat the oven to 350°F. Unwrap the dough; cut into ½-inch slices. Place the slices 2 inches apart on ungreased baking sheets.

4. Bake at 350°F for 13 to 15 minutes or until the edges are light golden brown. Cool on baking sheets 2 minutes. Transfer to wire racks, and cool completely (about 20 minutes).

✳ COOKIE ROOKIE ✳
Dough logs may be cut into ¼-inch-thick slices, if desired. The bake time remains the same. Makes about 6½ dozen.

LEMON-COCONUT SNOWBALLS

Lemon and coconut flavors add a new twist to the traditional wedding cookie.

HANDS-ON TIME 30 MINUTES   TOTAL TIME 1 HOUR 10 MINUTES   MAKES 24 COOKIES

1   cup unsalted butter, softened
2   cups powdered sugar
1   teaspoon coconut extract
1   teaspoon vanilla extract
2¼ cups all-purpose flour
1½ tablespoons grated lemon rind
½   teaspoon table salt
1   cup sweetened flaked coconut, lightly toasted
    Parchment paper

1. Beat the butter at medium speed with an electric mixer until creamy; gradually add ½ cup of the powdered sugar and the extracts, beating well. Add the flour, lemon rind, and salt, beating until combined. Stir in coconut. Cover and chill dough 30 minutes.

2. Preheat the oven to 350°F. Line baking sheets with parchment paper. Shape the dough into generous 1-inch balls; place 1 inch apart on prepared baking sheets. Bake at 350°F for 15 to 20 minutes or until golden on bottom but pale on the top. Transfer the cookies to wire racks; cool 5 minutes.

3. Place the remaining 1½ cups powdered sugar in a bowl, and roll the warm cookies in powdered sugar, coating well. Cool the cookies completely on wire racks (20 minutes). Roll the cooled cookies in powdered sugar again, coating well.

> ## * COOKIE ROOKIE *
> Don't be shy when rolling these yummy cookies in powdered sugar—the more powdered sugar, the bigger—and better—the snowball!

MISSISSIPPI MUD COOKIES

Rich chocolate and gooey marshmallows give these cake-derived treats their sweetness.

HANDS-ON TIME 25 MINUTES   TOTAL TIME 37 MINUTES   MAKES ABOUT 36 COOKIES

Parchment paper
- 1 **cup semisweet chocolate morsels**
- ½ **cup butter, softened**
- 1 **cup sugar**
- 2 **large eggs**
- 1 **teaspoon vanilla extract**
- 1½ **cups all-purpose flour**
- 1 **teaspoon baking powder**
- ½ **teaspoon table salt**
- 1 **cup chopped pecans**
- ½ **cup milk chocolate morsels**
- 108 **miniature marshmallows**

1. Preheat the oven to 350°F. Line baking sheets with parchment paper. Microwave semisweet chocolate morsels in a small microwave-safe glass bowl at HIGH 1 minute or until melted and smooth, stirring at 30-second intervals.

2. Beat the butter and sugar at medium speed with an electric mixer until creamy; add the eggs, 1 at a time, beating until blended after each addition. Beat in the vanilla and melted chocolate.

3. Stir together the flour, baking powder, and salt; gradually add to the chocolate mixture, beating until well blended. Stir in the chopped pecans and ½ cup milk chocolate morsels.

4. Drop the dough by heaping tablespoonfuls onto prepared baking sheets. Press 3 marshmallows into top of each cookie.

5. Bake at 350°F for 10 to 12 minutes or until set. Transfer to wire racks, and cool completely (about 20 minutes).

BROWNIES AND BARS

Leave these decadent brownies and chewy bars unattended, and they might disappear faster than you can say "Merry Christmas!"

PEPPERMINT-MARSHMALLOW BROWNIES

Dress up a premium brownie with fluffy marshmallow frosting and sparkling sugar.

HANDS-ON TIME 20 MINUTES   TOTAL TIME 1 HOUR 55 MINUTES   MAKES 16 BROWNIES

Cooking spray

1   (20-ounce) package dark chocolate brownie mix
½   cup canola oil
1   large egg
¼   cup water
1   cup powdered sugar
½   cup butter, softened
3   tablespoons marshmallow crème
¼   teaspoon peppermint extract
¼   cup peppermint sparkling sugar
    Crushed hard peppermint candies

1. Preheat the oven to 325°F. Coat a 9-inch square pan with cooking spray. Prepare the brownie mix batter according to package directions, using oil, egg, and ¼ cup water. Pour the batter into prepared pan. Bake at 325°F for 30 to 35 minutes or until a wooden pick inserted in the center comes out with a few moist crumbs. Cool completely in the pan on a wire rack (about 1 hour).

2. Beat the powdered sugar and butter at medium speed with an electric mixer until light and fluffy. Add the marshmallow crème and the peppermint extract, beating at low speed until blended. Spread the frosting evenly over cooled brownies. Sprinkle with the sparkling sugar and crushed candies. Cut into 4 rows by 4 rows.

NOTE: We tested with Betty Crocker Peppermint Sparkling Sugar.

PEPPERMINT-FUDGE BROWNIES

Use a pastry scraper, pizza cutter, or chef's knife to easily cut cooled brownies.

HANDS-ON TIME 20 MINUTES   TOTAL TIME 2 HOURS 20 MINUTES   MAKES 24 BROWNIES

Aluminum foil

Cooking spray

1½ cups butter, cut into pieces

1 (10-ounce) package bittersweet chocolate morsels

1¼ cups sugar

2 teaspoons vanilla extract

¾ teaspoon peppermint extract

4 large eggs

1¾ cups all-purpose flour

2 teaspoons baking powder

1 teaspoon table salt

2 cups semisweet chocolate morsels

1 cup whipping cream

¾ cup crushed hard peppermint candies (about 30 candies)

1. Preheat the oven to 350°F. Line the bottom and sides of a 13- x 9-inch pan with aluminum foil, allowing 2 to 3 inches to extend over the sides; lightly coat the foil with cooking spray.

2. Microwave the butter and bittersweet chocolate morsels in a large microwave-safe bowl at HIGH 1 to 2 minutes, stirring once, until melted and smooth. Whisk in the sugar, vanilla, and peppermint extract. Add the eggs, 1 at a time, whisking well after each addition. Stir in the flour, baking powder, and salt until combined. Pour the batter into prepared pan.

3. Bake at 350°F for 28 minutes or until a wooden pick inserted in the center comes out with a few moist crumbs. Cool completely in pan on a wire rack (about 1 hour).

4. Microwave the semisweet chocolate morsels and whipping cream in a microwave-safe bowl at HIGH 1 to 2 minutes, stirring once, until melted and smooth. Pour evenly over the brownies. Sprinkle with the peppermint candies. Chill 30 minutes or until set. Lift the brownies from pan, using the foil sides as handles. Gently remove the foil. Cut into 6 rows by 4 rows.

* COOKIE ROOKIE *

To easily crush peppermint candies, place them in a small zip-top plastic freezer bag, and smash with a rolling pin or the flat side of a meat mallet.

SO-GOOD BROWNIES

These brownies make a great base for experimenting with different flavors.

HANDS-ON TIME 10 MINUTES   TOTAL TIME 1 HOUR 50 MINUTES   MAKES 16 BROWNIES

Aluminum foil
Cooking spray
4   (1-ounce) unsweetened chocolate baking squares
¾   cup butter
1½ cups granulated sugar
½   cup firmly packed brown sugar
3   large eggs
1   cup all-purpose flour
1   teaspoon vanilla extract
⅛   teaspoon table salt

1. Preheat the oven to 350°F. Line the bottom and sides of an 8-inch square pan with aluminum foil, allowing 2 to 3 inches to extend over sides; lightly coat foil with cooking spray.

2. Microwave the chocolate squares and butter in a large microwave-safe bowl at HIGH 1½ to 2 minutes or until melted and smooth, stirring at 30-second intervals. Whisk in the sugars. Add the eggs, 1 at a time, whisking just until blended after each addition. Whisk in the flour, vanilla, and salt.

3. Pour the batter into the prepared pan.

4. Bake at 350°F for 40 to 44 minutes or until a wooden pick inserted in the center of the brownies comes out with a few moist crumbs. Cool completely on a wire rack (about 1 hour). Lift the brownies from the pan, using the foil sides as handles. Gently remove the foil, and cut into 4 rows by 4 rows.

FROSTED MOCHA ESPRESSO BROWNIES

Friends will rave over these brownies frosted with coffee-infused deliciousness.

HANDS-ON TIME 15 MINUTES   TOTAL TIME 1 HOUR 45 MINUTES   MAKES 24 BROWNIES

Cooking spray
1 (16.23-ounce) package fudge brownie mix
2 tablespoons instant espresso coffee granules or crystals
½ cup vegetable oil
¼ cup water
2 large eggs
¾ cup semisweet chocolate morsels
½ cup butter, softened
¾ teaspoon instant espresso coffee granules or crystals
1 teaspoon vanilla extract
2½ cups powdered sugar
2 teaspoons whipping cream

1. Preheat the oven to 350°F. Coat the bottom of a 13- x 9-inch pan with cooking spray.

2. Stir together the brownie mix, 2 tablespoons coffee granules, oil, water, and eggs in a large bowl with a wooden spoon. Stir in the chocolate morsels. Spread the batter in the prepared pan.

3. Bake at 350°F for 24 to 26 minutes or until the brownies begin to pull away from the sides of the pan. Cool completely in the pan on a wire rack (about 1 hour).

4. Beat the butter, ¾ teaspoon coffee granules, and vanilla at medium speed with an electric mixer until creamy. Add the powdered sugar, beating on low speed until blended. Beat in the whipping cream. Spread the frosting evenly over the cooled brownies. Cut into 6 rows by 4 rows.

AMARETTO-WALNUT BROWNIES

If desired, sift powdered sugar over brownie squares before serving.

HANDS-ON TIME 15 MINUTES   TOTAL TIME 7 HOURS 10 MINUTES   MAKES 15 BROWNIES

1   cup coarsely chopped walnuts, toasted
½   cup amaretto or almond-flavored liqueur
     Aluminum foil
     Cooking spray
1   cup butter
1   (8-ounce) unsweetened chocolate baking bar, chopped
5   large eggs
3½   cups sugar
¼   cup mocha-flavored instant coffee mix
1⅔   cups all-purpose flour
3   teaspoons vanilla extract
⅛   teaspoon table salt

1. Soak the chopped walnuts in the amaretto in a small bowl for 4 to 6 hours. Drain, discarding the amaretto. Set the walnuts aside.

2. Preheat the oven to 350°F. Line the bottom and sides of a 13- x 9-inch pan with aluminum foil, allowing 2 to 3 inches to extend over the sides. Coat the foil with cooking spray.

3. Melt the butter and chocolate in a 1-quart heavy saucepan over low, stirring frequently. Remove from the heat.

4. Beat the eggs, sugar, and coffee mix at medium-high speed with an electric mixer 8 minutes. Add the chocolate mixture, beating at low speed until blended. Gradually add the flour, vanilla, and salt, beating at low speed just until blended. Stir in the reserved soaked walnuts. Pour the batter into the prepared pan.

5. Bake at 350°F for 30 to 35 minutes. Cool completely in the pan on a wire rack (20 minutes). Lift the brownies from the pan, using the foil sides as handles; gently remove the foil. Cut into 5 rows by 3 rows.

NOTE: We tested with International Coffee Suisse Mocha.

SALTED ENGLISH TOFFEE BROWNIES

These fudge-style brownies are studded with toffee bits for a truly decadent dessert.

HANDS-ON TIME 20 MINUTES   TOTAL TIME 2 HOURS   MAKES 16 BROWNIES

Cooking spray
1 cup all-purpose flour
1⅓ cups granulated sugar
1 cup unsweetened cocoa
½ cup firmly packed brown sugar
¾ teaspoon baking powder
¼ teaspoon table salt
1 cup bittersweet chocolate chunks
½ cup butter
2 large eggs, lightly beaten
1 teaspoon vanilla extract
½ cup milk
1 (8-ounce) package toffee bits
¼ teaspoon sea salt flakes
Sea salt flakes (optional)

1. Preheat the oven to 350°F. Lightly coat a 9-inch square pan with cooking spray. Stir together the flour and next 5 ingredients in a large bowl.

2. Microwave ½ cup of the chocolate chunks and the butter in a microwave-safe bowl at HIGH 1 minute or until melted and smooth, stirring after 30 seconds. Gradually whisk in the eggs and vanilla. Stir the chocolate mixture into the flour mixture. Stir in the milk, remaining ½ cup chocolate chunks, and toffee bits.

3. Pour the batter into the prepared pan. Sprinkle evenly with ¼ teaspoon sea salt flakes.

4. Bake at 350°F for 40 minutes or until a wooden pick inserted in the center comes out with moist crumbs. Cool completely in the pan on a wire rack (about 1 hour). Sprinkle with additional sea salt flakes, if desired. Cut into 4 rows by 4 rows.

THAT'S A WRAP
Fill colorful take-out boxes with assorted cookies, brownies, and confections.

PECAN PIE BROWNIES

Take the frozen pie out of the freezer 2 hours beforehand so that it has time to thaw.

HANDS-ON TIME 25 MINUTES   TOTAL TIME 1 HOUR 15 MINUTES   MAKES 40 BROWNIES

Cooking spray
1   (2-pound) frozen pecan pie, thawed
½   cup butter
1¾ cups (11.5-ounce package) semisweet chocolate chunks
1   cup sugar
2   large eggs
1   cup milk
1½ cups all-purpose flour
1   teaspoon baking powder

1. Preheat the oven to 350°F. Coat a 13- x 9-inch pan with cooking spray. Cut the pie into cubes. Set aside.

2. Microwave the butter and chocolate chunks in a microwave-safe bowl at HIGH 1 minute. Stir and microwave 1 more minute. Stir until the mixture is smooth.

3. Beat the chocolate mixture, sugar, eggs, milk, and half of pie cubes at low speed with a heavy-duty electric stand mixer until blended.

4. Add the flour and baking powder, stirring with a wooden spoon until blended. Stir the remaining half of pie cubes into the batter. (Batter will be thick.) Spoon the batter into the prepared pan.

5. Bake at 350°F for 50 minutes. Cool completely in the pan on a wire rack (20 minutes). Cut into 40 triangles or squares.

CARAMEL-MOCHA-ALMOND BROWNIES

A sifter is ideal for dusting powdered sugar, but a fine-mesh strainer works great, too.

HANDS-ON TIME 20 MINUTES   TOTAL TIME 2 HOURS   MAKES 16 BROWNIES

Aluminum foil

Cooking spray

4 (1-ounce) unsweetened chocolate baking squares

¾ cup butter

1½ cups granulated sugar

½ cup firmly packed brown sugar

3 large eggs

1 cup all-purpose flour

1 teaspoon vanilla extract

Dash of table salt

1 cup mocha-flavored almonds, chopped

½ cup chopped chocolate-covered caramels

Powdered sugar

1. Preheat the oven to 350°F. Line the bottom and sides of an 8-inch square pan with aluminum foil, allowing 2 to 3 inches to extend over the sides; lightly coat the foil with cooking spray.

2. Microwave the chocolate squares and butter in a large microwave-safe bowl at HIGH 1½ to 2 minutes or until melted and smooth, stirring at 30-second intervals. Whisk in the sugars. Add the eggs, 1 at a time, whisking just until blended after each addition. Whisk in the flour, vanilla, and salt. Stir in the almonds and chopped caramels. Pour the batter into the prepared pan.

3. Bake at 350°F for 35 to 40 minutes or until a wooden pick inserted in the center comes out with several moist crumbs. Cool completely in the pan on a wire rack (about 1 hour).

4. Dust the brownies with powdered sugar. Lift the brownies from the pan, using the foil sides as handles. Gently remove the foil. Cut into 4 rows by 4 rows.

NOTE: We tested with Rolo caramel candies.

> ✳ **INGREDIENT SWAP** ✳
>
> If you can't find mocha-flavored almonds, use plain almonds, and add 2 teaspoons of instant coffee to the batter.

RED VELVET BROWNIES

The classic cake takes a bite-size detour.

HANDS-ON TIME 20 MINUTES   TOTAL TIME 1 HOUR 30 MINUTES   MAKES 16 BROWNIES

Aluminum foil
Cooking spray
1 (4-ounce) bittersweet chocolate baking bar, chopped
¾ cup butter
2 cups sugar
4 large eggs
1½ cups all-purpose flour
1 (1-ounce) bottle red liquid food coloring
1½ teaspoons baking powder
1 teaspoon vanilla extract
⅛ teaspoon table salt
Cream Cheese Frosting
White chocolate curls (optional)

CREAM CHEESE FROSTING

MAKES 1⅔ CUPS

1 (8-ounce) package cream cheese, softened
3 tablespoons butter, softened
1½ cups powdered sugar
⅛ teaspoon table salt
1 teaspoon vanilla extract

Beat the cream cheese and butter at medium speed with an electric mixer until creamy. Gradually add the powdered sugar and salt, beating until blended. Stir in the vanilla.

1. Preheat the oven to 350°F. Line a 9-inch square pan with aluminum foil, allowing 2 to 3 inches to extend over the sides; lightly coat the foil with cooking spray.

2. Microwave the chocolate and butter in a large microwave-safe bowl at HIGH 1½ to 2 minutes or until melted and smooth, stirring at 30-second intervals. Whisk in the sugar. Add the eggs, 1 at a time, whisking just until blended after each addition. Gently stir in the flour and next 4 ingredients. Pour the mixture into the prepared pan.

3. Bake at 350°F for 44 to 48 minutes or until a wooden pick inserted in the center comes out with a few moist crumbs. Cool completely in the pan on a wire rack (20 minutes).

4. Lift the brownies from the pan, using the foil sides as handles; gently remove the foil. Spread Cream Cheese Frosting on top of the brownies. Cut into 4 rows by 4 rows. Top with white chocolate curls, if desired.

NOTE: Line the pan with foil by trimming 2 long foil pieces to a 9-inch width. Fit strips, crossing each other, in the pan.

THAT'S A WRAP
Package cookies or brownies in a small wooden box lined with colorful, festive tissue paper.

PRETZEL-TOFFEE BLONDIES

This salty-sweet variation of a classic blond brownie will win over anyone.

HANDS-ON TIME 15 MINUTES   TOTAL TIME 1 HOUR 40 MINUTES   MAKES 16 BLONDIES

Cooking spray
½ cup butter, melted
1 cup packed brown sugar
1 teaspoon vanilla extract
⅛ teaspoon table salt
1 large egg
1 cup all-purpose flour
22 small pretzel twists, chopped
12 chocolate-covered small pretzel twists, chopped
4 (1.4-ounce) bars chocolate-covered English toffee candy, chopped

1. Preheat the oven to 350°F. Coat an 8-inch square pan with cooking spray. Stir together the butter and brown sugar in a medium bowl with a spoon until blended. Add the vanilla, salt, and egg; stir with a wire whisk until blended. Stir in the flour until blended. Stir in the pretzels and toffee candy. Pour into the prepared pan.

2. Bake at 350°F for 24 to 26 minutes or until set and a wooden pick inserted in the center comes out almost clean. Cool completely in the pan on a wire rack (about 1 hour). Cut into 4 rows by 4 rows. Store loosely covered.

BOURBON-PECAN BLONDIES

Brown sugar–laden, pecan-studded blondies get an extra boost of "yum" from bourbon.

HANDS-ON TIME 15 MINUTES   TOTAL TIME 1 HOUR 45 MINUTES   MAKES 32 BLONDIES

Cooking spray
- 1 cup butter, softened
- 2 cups firmly packed light brown sugar
- 2 large eggs
- ¼ cup bourbon
- 1½ teaspoons vanilla extract
- 2 cups all-purpose flour
- 1 teaspoon baking powder
- ½ teaspoon table salt
- 1 cup white chocolate morsels
- 1 cup coarsely chopped toasted pecans

1. Preheat the oven to 350°F. Lightly coat a 13- x 9-inch pan with cooking spray.

2. Beat the butter at medium speed with an electric mixer until creamy; gradually add the brown sugar, beating well. Add the eggs, 1 at a time, beating just until blended after each addition. Add the bourbon and vanilla, beating until blended.

3. Stir together the flour, baking powder, and salt; gradually add to the butter mixture, beating at low speed just until blended, stopping to scrape the bowl as needed. Stir in the white chocolate morsels and the pecans. Pour the batter into the prepared pan.

4. Bake at 350°F for 30 minutes or until a wooden pick inserted in the center comes out clean. Cool completely in the pan on a wire rack (about 1 hour). Cut into 8 rows by 4 rows.

> ### ✳ COOKIE ROOKIE ✳
> Mix the batters just until the flour is incorporated and the ingredients combine to avoid overworking the mixture, resulting in tough bars.

PEANUT BRITTLE BLONDIES

Dress up classic blondies with peanut brittle from your local candy shop.

HANDS-ON TIME 15 MINUTES   TOTAL TIME 1 HOUR 40 MINUTES   MAKES 24 BLONDIES

Shortening or cooking spray
2½ cups all-purpose flour
2½ teaspoons baking powder
½   teaspoon table salt
1½ cups packed light brown sugar
¾   cup butter
2   large eggs
3   cups coarsely crushed peanut brittle (about 14 ounces)
2   teaspoons vanilla extract

1. Preheat the oven to 350°F. Coat a 13- x 9-inch pan with shortening or cooking spray; lightly flour.

2. Stir together 2½ cups flour, baking powder, and salt.

3. Cook the brown sugar and butter in a 2-quart saucepan over medium, stirring frequently, until the butter is melted. Remove from heat; cool slightly. Add the eggs, 1 at a time, beating until blended after each addition. Stir in the flour mixture. Stir in the peanut brittle and vanilla. Press the dough into the prepared baking pan.

4. Bake at 350°F for 25 minutes or until golden. Cool completely in the pan on a wire rack (about 20 minutes). Cut into 6 rows by 4 rows.

> ## ☀ COOKIE ROOKIE ☀
> Store bars in airtight containers at room temperature up to 1 week. You may also freeze bars up to a month.

MAPLE-WALNUT BLONDIE STACKS

Consider using maple syrup from a local market for these adorable stacks.

HANDS-ON TIME 50 MINUTES   TOTAL TIME 2 HOURS 30 MINUTES   MAKES 36 BLONDIE STACKS

BLONDIE STACKS

Aluminum foil

Cooking spray

⅓ cup butter, softened

¾ cup firmly packed light brown sugar

2 large eggs

1 teaspoon vanilla extract

¾ cup all-purpose flour

¾ teaspoon baking powder

Dash of table salt

⅓ cup finely chopped toasted walnuts

⅓ cup coarsely crushed hard butter-toffee candies

MAPLE-BROWN SUGAR FROSTING

1 cup firmly packed light brown sugar

½ cup evaporated milk

⅓ cup butter

2 tablespoons light corn syrup

3 cups powdered sugar

2 tablespoons maple syrup

1 teaspoon vanilla extract

Additional coarsely crushed hard butter-toffee candies

Chopped toasted walnuts

1. Make Blondie Stacks: Preheat the oven to 350°F. Line bottom and sides of an 8-inch square pan with aluminum foil, allowing 2 to 3 inches to extend over sides; lightly coat foil with cooking spray.

2. Beat butter and brown sugar at medium speed with an electric mixer until creamy. Add eggs, 1 at a time, beating after each addition and scraping down sides of bowl. Stir in vanilla.

3. Stir together flour, baking powder, and salt in a small bowl, stirring well. Gradually add flour mixture to butter mixture, beating just until blended. Stir in ⅓ cup each walnuts and crushed toffee candies. Spread batter into prepared pan.

4. Bake at 350°F for 22 to 25 minutes or until a wooden pick inserted in center comes out with a few moist crumbs. Cool in pan on a wire rack 15 minutes.

5. Lift warm uncut blondies from pan, using foil sides as handles; place on a cutting board. Remove foil; cool completely (about 1 hour). Cut blondies into 4 equal portions. Cut each portion in half horizontally.

6. Make Maple-Brown Sugar Frosting: Stir together brown sugar, evaporated milk, butter, and corn syrup in a saucepan; cook over medium-low, stirring constantly, 7 minutes. Bring to a boil over medium-low; cook 5 minutes, stirring constantly. Remove from heat; stir in powdered sugar, syrup, and vanilla. Cool in pan on a wire rack 15 minutes. Transfer warm frosting mixture to a mixing bowl. Beat at medium-high speed with an electric mixer until smooth and spreading consistency (about 8 to 10 minutes).

7. Spread ¼ cup frosting onto each of 4 blondie portions; top with remaining 4 blondie portions. Cut each stack into 9 pieces. (We recommend using an electric knife.)

8. Spoon remaining frosting into a zip-top plastic freezer bag. Snip 1 corner of bag to make a small hole. Pipe about 1 teaspoon frosting onto each blondie stack. Sprinkle with additional crushed toffee and toasted walnuts.

BUTTERSCOTCH BARS

Butterscotch, boiled to the soft crack stage, must be "scotched," or cut, before it hardens.

HANDS-ON TIME 15 MINUTES   TOTAL TIME 1 HOUR 40 MINUTES   MAKES 16 BARS

Cooking spray
1 (15.25-ounce) yellow cake mix with pudding
2 large eggs
½ cup vegetable oil
½ teaspoon ground cinnamon
½ teaspoon ground nutmeg
1½ cups butterscotch morsels
1 cup cream cheese creamy ready-to-spread frosting
½ cup gingersnap cookies, coarsely crushed

1. Preheat the oven to 350°F. Coat the bottom and sides of a 9-inch square pan with cooking spray. Stir together the cake mix, eggs, oil, cinnamon, and nutmeg in a large bowl. Stir in 1 cup of the butterscotch morsels. Spread the batter in the prepared pan.

2. Bake at 350°F for 25 minutes or until set and lightly browned. Cool completely in the pan on a wire rack (1 hour).

3. Spread the frosting evenly over the cooled bars. Microwave the remaining ½ cup butterscotch morsels, uncovered, in a small microwave-safe bowl at HIGH 30 to 60 seconds or until melted and smooth, stirring at 30-second intervals. Spoon the melted morsels into a zip-top plastic freezer bag; seal the bag. Snip 1 corner of the bag to make a small hole; squeeze the bag to drizzle butterscotch over the frosting. Immediately sprinkle with crushed gingersnaps. Cut into 4 rows by 4 rows.

MAPLE-WALNUT BARS

This recipe calls for walnuts, but if you have other nuts on hand, give them a try!

HANDS-ON TIME 15 MINUTES   TOTAL TIME 2 HOURS 55 MINUTES   MAKES 16 BARS

Cooking spray
½ cup butter, softened
¼ cup granulated sugar
1 large egg yolk
1½ cups all-purpose flour
⅛ teaspoon table salt
½ cup maple syrup
⅓ cup packed brown sugar
¼ cup whipping cream
3 tablespoons butter
½ teaspoon vanilla extract
1½ cups coarsely chopped walnuts
⅓ cup semisweet chocolate morsels, melted

1. Preheat the oven to 350°F. Coat the bottom and sides of a 9-inch square pan with cooking spray.

2. Beat ½ cup butter, granulated sugar, and the egg yolk at low speed with an electric mixer 30 seconds, scraping the bowl occasionally. Add the flour and salt; beat until moist clumps form. Press the dough into the bottom and ½ inch up the sides of the prepared pan. Bake at 350°F for 15 to 18 minutes or until golden brown. Cool 5 minutes.

3. Heat the syrup, brown sugar, whipping cream, and 3 tablespoons butter to boiling in a 2-quart saucepan over medium, stirring constantly, until the butter is melted and the mixture is smooth. Remove from the heat; stir in the vanilla and walnuts. Pour the hot filling over the partially baked crust.

4. Bake at 350°F for 15 minutes or until the filling is bubbling in the center. Cool completely in the pan on a wire rack (20 minutes). Drizzle with the melted chocolate. Chill 1 hour. Cut into 4 rows by 4 rows.

> **✳ COOKIE ROOKIE ✳**
> Maple syrup offers sweet notes to these delicious seasonal bars. This natural, unrefined ingredient is one of the oldest forms of sweeteners.

MACADAMIA TURTLE BARS

Macadamia nuts replace the pecans in this delightfully salty-sweet take on turtle candy.

HANDS-ON TIME 25 MINUTES   TOTAL TIME 3 HOURS 25 MINUTES   MAKES 32 BARS

Aluminum foil
Cooking spray
2 cups all-purpose flour
½ cup powdered sugar
1½ cups butter
2 (6-ounce) jars dry-roasted macadamia nuts, coarsely chopped
1 cup firmly packed brown sugar
¾ cup whipping cream
½ cup light corn syrup
1 cup bittersweet chocolate morsels
1 tablespoon shortening

1. Preheat the oven to 350°F. Line the bottom and sides of a 13- x 9-inch pan with aluminum foil, allowing 2 to 3 inches to extend over the sides; lightly coat the foil with cooking spray.

2. Pulse the flour and powdered sugar in a food processor 3 or 4 times or until combined. Cut 1 cup of the butter into small pieces; add to the food processor. Pulse 10 times or until a crumbly dough forms. Press the dough into the bottom of the prepared pan.

3. Bake at 350°F for 20 minutes or until golden brown. Cool completely in the pan on a wire rack (about 1 hour). Sprinkle the macadamia nuts evenly over the crust.

4. Bring the brown sugar, whipping cream, corn syrup, and remaining ½ cup butter to a boil in a heavy medium saucepan over medium, stirring until the sugar dissolves and the butter melts. Cook until a candy thermometer registers 240°F (soft-ball stage), about 9 minutes. (Do not stir.) Remove from the heat; pour over the macadamia nuts in the pan. Cool completely in the pan on a wire rack (about 1 hour).

5. Microwave the chocolate morsels and shortening in a small microwave-safe bowl at HIGH 1 minute or until melted and smooth, stirring at 30-second intervals. Spoon the melted chocolate into a zip-top plastic freezer bag; seal the bag. Snip 1 corner of the bag to make a small hole; squeeze the bag to drizzle the chocolate over the bars in the pan. Chill 30 minutes or until the chocolate is firm.

6. Lift the bars from the pan, using the foil sides as handles. Gently remove the foil. Cut into 8 rows by 4 rows.

PEANUT BUTTER CRUNCH BARS

These made-from-scratch bars will remind you of a beloved candy bar—only better!

HANDS-ON TIME 25 MINUTES   TOTAL TIME 2 HOURS 55 MINUTES   MAKES 24 BARS

Cooking spray
1   cup sugar
⅓   cup water
⅓   cup light corn syrup
1   cup creamy peanut butter
1   cup semisweet chocolate
    morsels

1. Lightly coat an 8-inch square pan with cooking spray. Set aside.

2. Cook the sugar, ⅓ cup water, and corn syrup in a 2-quart heavy saucepan over medium, stirring constantly, until the sugar is dissolved. Heat to boiling. Cover and cook 2 to 3 minutes to wash the crystals from the sides of the pan. Uncover and boil 8 minutes, without stirring, to 310°F on a candy thermometer or until a small amount of the mixture dropped into a cup of very cold water separates into hard, brittle threads. (Watch carefully so the mixture does not burn.) Immediately remove from the heat.

3. Meanwhile, microwave the peanut butter in a large microwave-safe bowl, uncovered, at HIGH 45 seconds or until melted. Immediately pour the hot syrup mixture into the peanut butter, stirring constantly, just until blended. (Do not overstir.) Spread the mixture into the prepared pan. Cool 1 minute. With the tip of a sharp knife, score the bars into 6 rows by 4 rows. Cool completely (about 30 minutes).

4. Microwave the chocolate morsels in a microwave-safe bowl at HIGH 1 minute; stir until smooth. Spread the melted chocolate evenly over the peanut butter layer. Let stand until the chocolate is firm (about 2 hours). Cut into 6 rows by 4 rows. Store loosely covered.

> *✲ COOKIE ROOKIE ✲*
> Coat your measuring cup with cooking spray before portioning the peanut butter, and it will slide right out.

CHOCOLATE-PEPPERMINT COOKIE BARS

Crushed peppermints transform simple shortbread cookies into merry bars.

HANDS-ON TIME 1 HOUR   TOTAL TIME 2 HOURS 30 MINUTES   MAKES 48 BARS

2 cups all-purpose flour
¼ teaspoon baking powder
⅛ teaspoon table salt
1 cup butter, softened
¾ cup powdered sugar
2 teaspoons vanilla extract
½ teaspoon almond extract
  Waxed paper
  Parchment paper
¾ cup dark chocolate morsels
12 hard round peppermint candies, crushed

1. Stir together the flour, baking powder, and salt.

2. Beat the butter at medium speed with an electric mixer until creamy. Gradually add the powdered sugar, beating until smooth. Stir in the vanilla and almond extract until blended. Gradually add the flour mixture to the butter mixture, beating at low speed just until blended.

3. Divide the dough in half; flatten into rounds. Roll each round to ¼-inch thickness between 2 sheets of waxed paper. Place the dough on a baking sheet; chill 1 hour.

4. Preheat the oven to 350°F. Line baking sheets with parchment paper. Remove top sheet of the waxed paper from the dough; cut the dough into 48 (2½- x ¾-inch) rectangles. (Reroll the scraps once.) Place the bars 1 inch apart on the prepared baking sheets.

5. Bake at 350°F for 12 to 14 minutes or until the edges are golden. Cool on baking sheets 1 minute. Transfer to wire racks, and cool completely (about 20 minutes).

6. Microwave the chocolate morsels in a small microwave-safe bowl at HIGH about 1 minute or until the morsels are softened and can be stirred smooth. Drizzle the melted chocolate over the bars. Sprinkle with the crushed candies. Let stand 30 minutes or until set. Store the cookie bars in airtight containers at room temperature.

FRUITCAKE BARS

Loaded with dried fruits and roasted nuts, these bars are chock-full of tasty goodness.

HANDS-ON TIME 10 MINUTES   TOTAL TIME 1 HOUR 35 MINUTES   MAKES 20 BARS

Cooking spray

1 (16.5-ounce) package refrigerated sugar cookie dough

2 tablespoons all-purpose flour

2 tablespoons bourbon or brandy

¼ teaspoon ground cinnamon

⅛ teaspoon ground allspice

⅛ teaspoon ground nutmeg

½ cup chopped pecans

½ cup chopped pitted dates

½ cup chopped mixed candied fruit

1. Preheat the oven to 350°F. Coat the bottom and sides of a 9-inch square pan with cooking spray. Break up the cookie dough into a medium bowl. Stir in the flour, bourbon, cinnamon, allspice, and nutmeg until well blended. Stir in the pecans, dates, and candied fruit. Press into the prepared pan.

2. Bake at 350°F for 25 minutes or until golden brown. Cool completely in the pan on a wire rack (about 1 hour). Cut into 5 rows by 4 rows.

> ❋ **INGREDIENT SWAP** ❋
>
> Bourbon or brandy lend traditional fruitcake flavor to these bars. If you prefer to leave it out, substitute 1 teaspoon brandy extract, and omit the flour.

RUBY RED GRAPEFRUIT BARS

For snowy decoration, place a stencil on each bar before dusting with powdered sugar.

HANDS-ON TIME 18 MINUTES   TOTAL TIME 2 HOURS 28 MINUTES   MAKES 24 BARS

1   cup butter, softened
½   cup powdered sugar
1½ cups all-purpose flour
⅛   teaspoon table salt
2   cups granulated sugar
⅓   cup all-purpose flour
½   teaspoon baking powder
1   tablespoon grated red
    grapefruit rind
¾   cup fresh red grapefruit juice
6   large eggs
    Christmas stencils (optional)
    Powdered sugar

1. Preheat the oven to 350°F. Beat the butter at medium speed with an electric mixer until creamy; gradually add ½ cup powdered sugar, beating until blended. Add 1½ cups flour and salt; beat until blended. Press the mixture into the bottom of an ungreased 13- x 9-inch baking pan. Bake at 350°F for 18 minutes or until lightly browned. Cool 10 minutes.

2. Meanwhile, stir together the granulated sugar, ⅓ cup flour, and baking powder in a medium bowl. Whisk together the rind, juice, and eggs; add to the flour mixture, stirring until well blended. Pour over the crust.

3. Bake at 350°F for 30 minutes or until set. Cool completely in the pan on a wire rack (about 1½ hours). Cut into 6 rows by 4 rows; place Christmas stencils over each square, if desired, and dust with powdered sugar.

> ✳ **COOKIE ROOKIE** ✳
> If you would like your bars pink like a fresh-cut grapefruit, add a drop or two of red food coloring to the filling before baking.

WHITE CHOCOLATE-CRANBERRY BARS

Creamy white chocolate complements the sweet dried cranberries in this heavenly bar.

HANDS-ON TIME 10 MINUTES   TOTAL TIME 2 HOURS 45 MINUTES   MAKES 24 BARS

Aluminum foil

Cooking spray

1 cup butter, softened

2 cups packed brown sugar

2 large eggs

2 teaspoons vanilla extract

2 cups all-purpose flour

½ teaspoon baking powder

¼ teaspoon table salt

1 cup white chocolate morsels

1 cup chopped walnuts

¾ cup sweetened dried cranberries

1. Preheat the oven to 350°F. Line the bottom and sides of a 13- x 9-inch pan with aluminum foil, allowing 2 to 3 inches to extend over the sides. Coat the foil with cooking spray.

2. Beat the butter and brown sugar at medium speed with an electric mixer until well blended. Beat in the eggs and vanilla. Beat in the flour, baking powder, and salt, beating at low speed until blended. Stir in the morsels, walnuts, and cranberries. Spread in the prepared pan.

3. Bake at 350°F for 30 to 35 minutes or until golden brown and set. Cool completely in the pan on a wire rack (about 20 minutes). Lift the bars from the pan, using the foil sides as handles; gently remove the foil. Cut into 6 rows by 4 rows.

WHITE CHOCOLATE CHEESECAKE BARS

For an elegant garnish, top this cheesecake dessert with fresh berries and mint.

HANDS-ON TIME 30 MINUTES   TOTAL TIME 4 HOURS 40 MINUTES   MAKES 16 BARS

Shortening or cooking spray

1¼ cups thin chocolate wafer cookies, crushed

6 tablespoons butter, melted

2 (8-ounce) packages cream cheese, softened

½ cup sugar

1 teaspoon vanilla extract

2 large eggs

1 (6-ounce) package white chocolate baking bars, chopped

1 tablespoon all-purpose flour

Fresh raspberries and mint leaves (optional)

1. Preheat the oven to 350°F. Coat an 8-inch square pan with shortening or cooking spray. Stir together the crushed cookies and butter in a small bowl. Press into the bottom of the pan. Bake at 350°F for 10 minutes. Cool completely (about 20 minutes).

2. Reduce the oven temperature to 325°F. Beat the cream cheese, sugar, and vanilla in a large bowl at medium speed with an electric mixer until light and fluffy. Beat in the eggs, 1 at a time, just until blended. Stir together the white chocolate and flour in a small bowl; fold into the cream cheese mixture. Spread the batter over the crust.

3. Bake at 325°F for 28 to 30 minutes or until the edges are set but the center still jiggles slightly. Cool completely in pan on a wire rack (about 1 hour). Chill 2 hours before serving. Cut into 4 rows by 4 rows. Top each bar with raspberries and mint leaves, if desired.

> *** COOKIE ROOKIE ***
> For a quick way to crush the chocolate wafers, pulse them in a food processor until desired texture.

TIRAMISÙ LAYER BARS

Rich mascarpone cheese and coffee-flavored liqueur combine to make a luscious bar.

HANDS-ON TIME 35 MINUTES   TOTAL TIME 3 HOURS 45 MINUTES   MAKES 24 BARS

Aluminum foil

Cooking spray

1½ cups thin chocolate wafer cookies, crushed

6 tablespoons butter, melted

½ cup strong brewed coffee (room temperature)

¼ cup granulated sugar

2 tablespoons coffee-flavored liqueur

1 (10.75-ounce) package frozen pound cake loaf, thawed

1 cup whipping cream

¼ cup powdered sugar

1 (8-ounce) container mascarpone cheese

1 tablespoon unsweetened cocoa

1. Preheat the oven to 350°F. Line a 9-inch square pan with aluminum foil, allowing 2 to 3 inches to extend over the sides; coat the foil with cooking spray. Stir together the cookie crumbs and butter in a medium bowl. Press into the prepared pan. Bake at 350°F for 10 minutes. Cool completely (about 30 minutes).

2. Meanwhile, heat the coffee and granulated sugar in a 1-quart saucepan to boiling over medium-high, stirring occasionally. Remove from heat. Cool completely (about 30 minutes). Stir in the liqueur.

3. Cut the pound cake into 13 (½-inch) slices; trim to level top of each slice.

4. Beat the whipping cream and powdered sugar in a chilled large bowl at high speed with an electric mixer until soft peaks form. Add the mascarpone cheese; beat at medium speed until stiff peaks form. (Do not overbeat.) Spread half of the whipped cream mixture over the crust in the pan. Top with the pound cake slices, fitting snugly together. Brush with the coffee syrup mixture until absorbed. Spread with the remaining whipped cream mixture. Sift or sprinkle cocoa over top.

5. Cover; chill 2 hours. Lift the bars from the pan, using the foil sides as handles; gently remove the foil. Cut into 6 rows by 4 rows. Store covered in the refrigerator.

ITALIAN RAINBOW BARS

The colors of the cake-like layers in these bars evoke Italy's flag and the holiday season.

HANDS-ON TIME 30 MINUTES   TOTAL TIME 2 HOURS 45 MINUTES   MAKES 32 BARS

Cooking spray
Parchment paper

2	cups all-purpose flour
¼	teaspoon baking powder
¼	teaspoon table salt
1¼	cups butter, softened
1	cup sugar
1	(7-ounce) package almond paste, crumbled
½	teaspoon almond extract
3	large eggs
¼	teaspoon green food coloring paste
½	teaspoon red food coloring paste
⅓	cup seedless raspberry jam
8	ounces bittersweet baking chocolate, chopped
¼	cup whipping cream

1. Preheat the oven to 350°F. Coat a 13- x 9-inch pan with cooking spray; line with parchment paper, leaving 1 inch of paper overhanging at 2 opposite sides of pan. Coat the paper with cooking spray.

2. Stir together the flour, baking powder, and salt in a small bowl until blended. Beat the butter and next 3 ingredients in a medium bowl at medium speed with an electric mixer 5 minutes or until light and fluffy. Beat in the eggs, 1 at a time, until blended. Beat in the flour mixture on low speed. Spread one-third of the batter (1½ cups) evenly in the prepared pan. (Layer will be very thin.) Freeze 5 minutes.

3. Stir the green food coloring into one-third (1½ cups) of the batter in another small bowl. Gently spread over the batter in the pan. Freeze 5 minutes. Stir the red food coloring into the remaining batter in a separate small bowl. Gently spread over the green batter.

4. Bake at 350°F for 24 to 28 minutes or until a wooden pick inserted in the center comes out clean. Cool completely in the pan on a wire rack (about 1 hour). Spread the jam over the bars. Microwave the chocolate and whipping cream in a microwave-safe bowl at HIGH about 1 minute, stirring until smooth. Spread the chocolate mixture over the jam. Chill 30 minutes or until the chocolate is set. Use the paper to lift the bars out of the pan; gently remove the paper. Trim the edges, if desired. Cut into 8 rows by 4 rows. Store loosely covered.

THAT'S A WRAP

Lift the uncut bars out of the pan, cut in half, and give each half as a mega bar. Line the pan with foil or parchment paper to make it easy to lift the bars out of the pan.

CONFECTIONS

The best sweets come in small packages, and these bites pack tons of flavor. Share these tiny treats to spread the seasonal joy.

GERMAN CHOCOLATE CAKE TRUFFLES

Call these truffles or cake balls; they're easy to make, and everyone will love them.

HANDS-ON TIME 45 MINUTES   TOTAL TIME 3 HOURS 20 MINUTES   MAKES 102 TRUFFLES

Cooking spray
1   (18.25-ounce) package German chocolate cake mix
    Waxed paper
1   (16-ounce) container milk chocolate ready-to-spread frosting
2   cups sweetened flaked coconut, toasted
1¾ cups toasted finely chopped pecans
4   (7-ounce) containers milk chocolate dipping chocolate
    Candy dipping fork
    Paper or aluminum foil baking cups

1. Lightly coat a 13- x 9-inch pan with cooking spray. Prepare the cake mix according to the package directions, and bake in the prepared pan. Cool completely in the pan (about 30 minutes).

2. Line baking sheets with waxed paper. Crumble the cake into a large bowl. Scoop the frosting by spoonfuls over the cake crumbs. Sprinkle with 1 cup each of the coconut and pecans; stir gently just until thoroughly blended. Using a cookie scoop, scoop the cake mixture into 1¼-inch balls; roll in hands, and place the balls (spaced evenly apart) on prepared baking sheets. Cover and chill 1 hour.

3. While the cake balls chill, stir together the remaining 1 cup coconut and ¾ cup pecans; stir well. Melt the dipping chocolate, 1 container at a time, according to package directions; dip the chilled balls in the melted chocolate, using a candy dipping fork and allowing excess chocolate to drip off. Place the coated truffles on prepared baking sheets. Sprinkle the tops with the coconut-pecan mixture; chill 30 minutes or until set. Place each truffle in a paper baking cup.

DARK CHOCOLATE TRUFFLES WITH FLEUR DE SEL

These rich truffles have a hard chocolate coating that lends some crunch.

HANDS-ON TIME 30 MINUTES   TOTAL TIME 4 HOURS 30 MINUTES   MAKES ABOUT 24 TRUFFLES

8   ounces bittersweet chocolate, chopped
¼   cup sugar
1   tablespoon water
⅔   cup whipping cream
¼   teaspoon fleur de sel or coarse sea salt
½   cup Dutch process cocoa, sifted
12   ounces bittersweet chocolate, broken into pieces
     Parchment paper
     Additional fleur de sel or coarse sea salt

1. Microwave 8 ounces bittersweet chocolate in a microwave-safe bowl at HIGH 1 minute or until melted.

2. Combine the sugar and 1 tablespoon water in a small heavy saucepan; cook over medium until the sugar dissolves, stirring gently. Continue to simmer, without stirring, about 7 minutes or until the syrup is golden, brushing down the sides of the pan with a pastry brush dipped in water; remove pan from heat. Carefully add the cream. (Mixture will bubble.) Return the pan to low, and simmer, stirring until smooth. Stir in the fleur de sel. Remove from the heat. Add the cream mixture to the melted chocolate; stir until smooth, and cool completely (about 15 minutes). Cover and chill 3 hours or until firm.

3. Place the cocoa in a bowl. Shape the chocolate mixture into 1-inch balls. (We used a 1-inch ice-cream scoop.) Roll the balls in the cocoa. Place the truffle balls on a baking sheet; chill until firm.

4. Place 12 ounces bittersweet chocolate in the top of a double boiler over simmering water until a thermometer inserted into the chocolate registers 115°F. Remove the top insert; working quickly, dip the truffles in the melted chocolate, coating completely. Lift out the truffles with a candy dipping fork, letting excess chocolate drip off. Tilt the double boiler insert, if needed, to make dipping and coating easier. Return the top insert to the heat every few minutes to keep the chocolate at 115°F. Transfer the truffles to parchment paper. Sprinkle the truffles lightly with additional fleur de sel. Let stand 30 minutes or until the chocolate coating is set.

SNICKERDOODLE TRUFFLES

These truffles transform a popular cinnamon-sugar cookie into a bite-size treat.

HANDS-ON TIME 35 MINUTES   TOTAL TIME 4 HOURS 20 MINUTES   MAKES 26 TRUFFLES

1   (16-ounce) package refrigerated sugar cookie dough
3   tablespoons sugar
1½ teaspoons ground cinnamon
    Parchment paper
1   (8-ounce) package cream cheese, cut into cubes
10 ounces vanilla candy coating, chopped

1. Preheat the oven to 350°F. Shape the dough into 1-inch balls. Stir together half each of the sugar and cinnamon in a small bowl. Roll the dough balls in the cinnamon-sugar mixture. Place the balls about 2 inches apart on an ungreased baking sheet.

2. Bake at 350°F for 10 to 14 minutes or until the edges are lightly browned. Cool on baking sheet 1 minute. Transfer to a wire rack, and cool completely (about 20 minutes).

3. Line a baking sheet with parchment paper. Process cooled cookies in a food processor until fine crumbs form. Add the cream cheese. Pulse until the mixture is smooth. Shape into 1-inch balls; place on the prepared baking sheet. Chill 3 hours.

4. Microwave the candy coating in a microwave-safe bowl at MEDIUM 1 minute, and then in 15-second intervals, until melted; stir until smooth. Stir together the remaining sugar and cinnamon in a small bowl. Dip the chilled truffles in the melted coating; letting the excess drip off. Roll in the cinnamon-sugar. Return to the baking sheet; let stand 30 minutes or until set.

THAT'S A WRAP

Make truffle "pops" by punching a hole in the bottom of paper candy cups. Insert a lollipop stick through the hole and then into the truffle. Tie thin ribbon around the stick.

BRANDIED CHERRY BROWNIE BITES

Dress up a boxed brownie mix with a few extra mix-ins to make these candy treats.

HANDS-ON TIME 30 MINUTES   TOTAL TIME 3 HOURS 20 MINUTES   MAKES 48 BITES

Cooking spray
1 cup dried cherries
⅓ cup brandy
1 (19.9-ounce) package dark chocolate fudge brownie mix
¾ cup toasted, skins removed, chopped hazelnuts
Waxed paper
12 ounces semisweet baking chocolate, chopped
½ cup hazelnut spread with cocoa
Candy dipping fork

1. Preheat the oven to 350°F. Coat a 9-inch square pan with cooking spray. Heat cherries and brandy in a 1-quart saucepan to simmering over medium. Remove from the heat; let stand 15 minutes. Strain the cherries; reserve the brandy.

2. Make the brownie mix according to package directions. Stir in the cherries, reserved brandy, and ½ cup of the hazelnuts. Pour into the prepared pan.

3. Bake at 350°F for 30 to 35 minutes or until a wooden pick inserted in the center comes out clean. Cool in the pan on a wire rack 30 minutes. Chill 1 hour.

4. Line a baking sheet with waxed paper. Scoop out the brownies using a spoon, and shape into 1-inch balls; place on the prepared baking sheet.

5. Microwave the baking chocolate in a microwave-safe bowl, uncovered, at HIGH 1 minute or until melted, stirring after 30 seconds. Stir in the hazelnut spread until well blended. Using a candy dipping fork, dip the brownie balls, 1 at a time, into the chocolate mixture, letting the excess drip off. Return to baking sheet. Sprinkle with the remaining ¼ cup hazelnuts. Chill 30 minutes or until set.

THAT'S A WRAP

Bundle these treats in a holiday carton or, for a clever way to package them, place individual candies in shot glasses.

BOURBON SHORTBREAD TRUFFLES

These gussied up, no-bake treats offer a powerful punch of flavor in a small bite.

HANDS-ON TIME 30 MINUTES   TOTAL TIME 3 HOURS 30 MINUTES   MAKES 36 TRUFFLES

12   ounces bittersweet baking chocolate, chopped
1½   tablespoons cold butter, cut into small pieces
2   teaspoons vanilla extract
9   tablespoons whipping cream
¼   cup bourbon
1   (5.3-ounce) package pure butter shortbread cookies, crushed
2   cups finely chopped salted roasted pecans
Waxed paper

1. Stir together the chocolate, butter, and vanilla in a large microwave-safe bowl.

2. Cook the whipping cream and bourbon over medium 3 to 4 minutes or until hot but not boiling. (Mixture will steam, and bubbles will form around the edge of the pan.) Pour over the chocolate mixture. Let stand 1 minute.

3. Stir the chocolate mixture until melted and smooth. (If mixture doesn't melt completely, microwave at HIGH 30 seconds.) Stir in the crushed cookies. Cover and chill 3 hours or until firm. (Mixture can be prepared and refrigerated up to 2 days ahead.)

4. Place the chopped pecans in a bowl. Shape the chocolate mixture into 1-inch balls (about 2 teaspoons per ball). Roll the balls in chopped pecans. Place on baking sheets lined with waxed paper. Chill 1 hour. Store tightly covered in the refrigerator up to 5 days.

MOCHA BALLS

Use a sturdy wooden pick to dip hand-shaped balls into the melted chocolate.

HANDS-ON TIME 25 MINUTES   TOTAL TIME 55 MINUTES   MAKES 32 BALLS

Parchment paper

56   vanilla wafers, crushed (about 1 [11-ounce] box)

1   cup chopped almonds, toasted

½   cup powdered sugar

2   tablespoons unsweetened cocoa

4½   teaspoons light corn syrup

6   tablespoons coffee liqueur

3   cups semisweet chocolate morsels

Roasted coffee beans (optional)

Line a baking sheet with parchment paper. Stir together the wafers and next 5 ingredients; shape into 32 balls. Microwave the chocolate in a microwave-safe bowl at HIGH 30 seconds; stir. Microwave 20 more seconds or until smooth, stirring once. Dip the balls in the melted chocolate. Place on the prepared pan. Decorate each ball with a coffee bean, if desired. Chill 30 minutes or until set.

MINTED WHITE CHOCOLATE BALLS

Prepare the recipe as directed, substituting pecans for the almonds, 6 tablespoons peppermint schnapps for the coffee liqueur, and white chocolate morsels for the chocolate morsels. Sprinkle with crushed hard peppermint candies immediately after coating with white chocolate.

CHOCOLATE STOUT TRUFFLES

Dark chocolate flavored with stout beer and rolled in sweet cocoa creates irresistible bites.

HANDS-ON TIME 30 MINUTES   TOTAL TIME 3 HOURS 45 MINUTES   MAKES 43 TRUFFLES

1   cup dark stout beer
16 ounces dark baking
     chocolate, chopped
     Waxed paper
⅓ cup powdered sugar
2   tablespoons unsweetened
     baking cocoa

1. Microwave the beer, uncovered, in a microwave-safe bowl at HIGH 1 minute or until hot. Place 16 ounces of the dark chocolate in a heatproof bowl. Pour the hot beer into the dark chocolate; let stand 1 minute. Stir until smooth. Cover and chill 3 hours or until firm.

2. Line a baking sheet with waxed paper. Scoop rounded teaspoonfuls of the chocolate mixture; shape into 1-inch balls. Place on the prepared baking sheet. Chill 15 minutes or until firm.

3. Stir together the powdered sugar and cocoa. Dip the truffles, 1 at a time, in the cocoa mixture to coat completely. Store tightly covered at room temperature up to 3 days.

✻ COOKIE ROOKIE ✻
When rolling these truffles, use rubber gloves to avoid messy hands.

CAPPUCCINO-WALNUT TOFFEE

Some butters have a higher water content. Residual water will affect the smooth texture.

HANDS-ON TIME 30 MINUTES   TOTAL TIME 2 HOURS 15 MINUTES   MAKES ABOUT 2 POUNDS CANDY

Cooking spray
2 cups walnuts, chopped
1¼ cups butter
1 cup granulated sugar
⅓ cup firmly packed light brown sugar
1 tablespoon dark unsulphured molasses
2 teaspoons instant espresso
½ teaspoon ground cinnamon
¼ teaspoon table salt
⅓ cup water
1 cup milk chocolate morsels
1 cup white chocolate morsels

1. Preheat the oven to 350°F. Coat a 15- x 10-inch jelly-roll pan with cooking spray.

2. Bake the walnuts at 350°F in a single layer in a separate shallow pan 8 to 10 minutes or until toasted and fragrant, stirring halfway through. Cool completely 30 minutes.

3. Melt the butter in a 3½-quart heavy saucepan over medium; stir in the granulated sugar, next 5 ingredients, and ⅓ cup water. Cook, stirring constantly, until a candy thermometer registers 290°F (soft-crack stage), about 20 minutes. Remove the pan from heat, and stir in the toasted walnuts. Quickly pour the mixture into the prepared pan, and spread into an even layer. Immediately sprinkle the milk chocolate and white chocolate morsels over the top; let stand 5 minutes. Swirl the chocolate using an off-set spatula. Cover and chill until firm (about 1 hour). Break the toffee into 1½- to 2-inch pieces. Store in an airtight container in the refrigerator up to 7 days. Serve cold or at room temperature.

NOTE: We tested with Land O'Lakes Butter.

> **✳ COOKIE ROOKIE ✳**
> Check the accuracy of your candy thermometer. Heat a saucepan of water to boiling with the thermometer clipped onto the side, and boil 2 minutes. The thermometer should read 212°F.

BUTTERY ALMOND TOFFEE

This crisp candy melts into buttery richness in your mouth.

HANDS-ON TIME 25 MINUTES   TOTAL TIME 2 HOURS 5 MINUTES   MAKES ABOUT 2½ POUNDS CANDY

1 cup chopped whole natural almonds (with skin)
2 tablespoons unsalted butter, melted
1 cup unsalted butter
   Plastic wrap
2 cups sugar
¼ cup water
¼ cup light corn syrup
½ teaspoon table salt
1 teaspoon vanilla extract
   Cooking spray
   Parchment paper
1 (12-ounce) package semisweet chocolate morsels

COFFEE TOFFEE
MAKES ABOUT 2 POUNDS CANDY

Stir together 1½ teaspoons instant espresso granules with ¼ cup water when adding water as recipe directs. Microwave the candy mixture at HIGH as recipe directs, microwaving only 9 minutes (instead of 10) at the end of Step 2. Sprinkle ½ cup chopped chocolate-covered coffee beans in addition to chopped almonds over the melted chocolate topping, if desired.

1. Preheat the oven to 350°F. Stir together the almonds and 2 tablespoons melted butter on a jelly-roll pan. Bake at 350°F for 8 minutes; stir and bake 2 more minutes. Drain on paper towels.

2. Coat a baking sheet with cooking spray and line with parchment paper. Set aside. Place 1 cup butter in a large microwave-safe bowl. Cover with plastic wrap, and microwave at HIGH 1 minute. Add the sugar, water, corn syrup, and salt. Cover and microwave at HIGH 3 minutes. Uncover, stir gently, and microwave at HIGH 10 minutes or until golden. Stir in the vanilla. Pour the candy mixture onto the prepared pan, quickly spreading candy to ¼-inch thickness.

3. Sprinkle the chocolate morsels over the toffee; let stand 1 minute or until the chocolate begins to melt. Spread the chocolate evenly over the candy; sprinkle with the toasted almonds, pressing gently with fingertips. Cool completely (about 30 minutes). Chill 1 hour or until firm. Break the toffee into 1½- to 2-inch pieces. Store in an airtight container.

MACADAMIA-TOFFEE BRITTLE

Creamy, rich macadamia nuts combine with buttery toffee to create a delicious holiday gift.

HANDS-ON TIME 20 MINUTES   TOTAL TIME 1 HOUR 10 MINUTES   MAKES 26 PIECES

Cooking spray
1 cup sugar
½ cup light corn syrup
½ teaspoon kosher salt
2 cups coarsely chopped macadamia nuts
1 tablespoon butter, cut into small pieces
1 teaspoon baking soda
1 teaspoon vanilla extract
½ cup toffee bits
¾ cup milk chocolate morsels, melted

1. Coat a 15- x 10-inch jelly-roll pan or large baking sheet with cooking spray. Set aside.

2. Stir together the sugar, corn syrup, and salt in a 2-quart microwave-safe bowl. Microwave, uncovered, at HIGH 4 minutes or until the mixture is bubbling. Stir in the macadamia nuts and butter. Microwave at HIGH 3 to 5 minutes or until golden brown.

3. Stir in the baking soda and vanilla. (Mixture will bubble.) Immediately pour into the prepared pan, spreading to ¼-inch thickness with a lightly greased spatula.

4. Sprinkle the toffee bits over the top. Spoon the melted morsels into a zip-top plastic freezer bag; seal the bag. Snip off 1 corner of the bag to make a small hole. Squeeze the bag to drizzle chocolate over the brittle. Cool completely (about 30 minutes). Chill 20 minutes or until the chocolate sets. Break into 1½- to 2-inch pieces.

✳ INGREDIENT SWAP ✳

This simple microwave nut brittle would be equally delicious with any blend of salted roasted nuts. For purists, omit the toffee bits.

PISTACHIO-CRANBERRY BRITTLE

Fill pretty glass jars with brittle pieces for an easy yet beautiful gift.

HANDS-ON TIME 20 MINUTES   TOTAL TIME 1 HOUR 20 MINUTES   MAKES 2¾ POUNDS CANDY

Cooking spray
2   cups sugar
1   cup light corn syrup
    Plastic wrap
1   cup pistachios, toasted
1   cup sweetened dried
    cranberries
3   tablespoons butter,
    cut into pieces
1   teaspoon baking soda
1   teaspoon vanilla extract

PUMPKIN SEED BRITTLE

MAKES ABOUT 1½ POUNDS CANDY

Substitute 1 cup shelled, roasted and salted pumpkin seeds (pepitas) for pistachios and cranberries. Stir in the pumpkin seeds at the start of Step 2. Proceed with recipe as directed, microwaving at HIGH 7 to 8 minutes in Step 2.

1. Coat a 15- x 10-inch jelly-roll pan or large baking sheet with cooking spray.

2. Stir together the sugar and corn syrup in a large microwave-safe bowl. Cover with plastic wrap, and microwave at HIGH 4 minutes.

3. Uncover and microwave at HIGH 7 to 8 more minutes or until mixture is light golden brown; stir in the pistachios and cranberries. Microwave, uncovered, at HIGH 1 minute or just until the mixture returns to a boil. Quickly stir in the butter, baking soda, and vanilla. (The candy mixture will foam.)

4. Quickly pour the candy mixture onto the prepared pan, spreading to the edges of the pan using a buttered metal spoon or spatula. Cool completely (about 30 minutes). Chill 1 hour until firm. Break the candy into 1½- to 2-inch pieces. Store in an airtight container.

NOTE: We tested using an 1100-watt microwave oven.

WHITE CHOCOLATE-PEPPERMINT JUMBLES

Using a slow cooker allows for a hands-off candy creation without sacrificing flavor.

HANDS-ON TIME 15 MINUTES   TOTAL TIME 2 HOURS 45 MINUTES   MAKES 96 CANDIES

2   (16-ounce) packages vanilla bark coating
1   (12-ounce) package white chocolate morsels
1   (6-ounce) package white chocolate baking squares
3   tablespoons shortening
1   (16-ounce) package pretzel nuggets
1   (8-ounce) package animal-shaped crackers (3 cups)
1   cup hard peppermint candies, coarsely crushed
    Waxed paper

1. Add the first 4 ingredients to a 6-quart electric slow cooker. Cook, covered, at LOW 1½ hours or until the vanilla bark and chocolate look very soft. Uncover and stir until smooth. Stir in the pretzels, crackers, and crushed peppermint candies.

2. Drop the mixture by heaping tablespoonfuls onto waxed paper. Let stand 1 hour or until firm.

> ✳ **COOKIE ROOKIE** ✳
> Waxed paper is nonstick and moisture resistant. Use it to cover countertops when measuring dry ingredients to ensure no mess and no waste.

CHOCOLATE-PEANUT BUTTER-PRETZEL BITES

These candies utilize everything but the kitchen sink for a sweet, salty, and crunchy bite.

HANDS-ON TIME 15 MINUTES   TOTAL TIME 45 MINUTES   MAKES 11 CUPS

2½ cups chocolate-flavored candy melts

3 ounces bittersweet chocolate, chopped

Waxed paper

2 (8-ounce) packages peanut butter-filled pretzel sandwiches

1 cup cocktail peanuts, finely chopped

¾ cup peanut butter morsels

1½ tablespoons shortening

1. Microwave the candy melts and bittersweet chocolate in a large microwave-safe bowl at MEDIUM 2 to 3 minutes or until melted and smooth, stirring at 1-minute intervals.

2. Line baking sheets with waxed paper. Add the pretzel sandwiches to the melted chocolate, tossing well to coat. Using a fork, transfer the coated pretzels onto the prepared baking sheets, allowing the excess chocolate to drip back into the bowl. Sprinkle the dipped pretzels with the nuts.

3. Microwave the peanut butter morsels and shortening in a 1-cup glass measuring cup at HIGH 30 seconds or until the morsels are very soft. Stir until smooth. Spoon the mixture into a zip-top plastic freezer bag. (Do not seal.) Snip 1 corner of the bag to make a small hole. Squeeze the bag to pipe the peanut butter mixture over the coated pretzels. Chill 30 minutes or until chocolate is firm.

NOTE: We tested with Snyder's Peanut Butter Pretzel Sandwiches.

SEA TURTLES

Top these candies with finishing salt to intensify the chocolate and caramel flavors.

HANDS-ON TIME 20 MINUTES   TOTAL TIME 1 HOUR 40 MINUTES   MAKES 30 CANDIES

4   cups chopped pecans
2   (11-ounce) packages caramel bits
¼   cup whipping cream
2   teaspoons vanilla extract
2   (4-ounce) bittersweet chocolate baking bars, chopped
¼   cup shortening
2   (4-ounce) white chocolate baking bars, chopped
2   tablespoons coarse sea salt (optional)

1. Preheat the oven to 350°F. Place the pecans in a single layer in a 15- x 10-inch jelly-roll pan. Bake at 350°F for 5 to 6 minutes or until toasted and fragrant, stirring halfway through. Cool completely.

2. Melt the caramel bits and cream in a heavy saucepan over medium, stirring until smooth. Remove from the heat; stir in the vanilla.

3. Using 1 tablespoon of the caramel mixture at a time, spoon circles close together over the pecans, covering the entire pan. Chill 10 minutes or until the caramel is firm. Carefully lift the candies, and transfer to a serving platter, reserving the remaining pecans in the pan. Redistribute the pecans on the pan into a solid single layer. Repeat the procedure with the remaining caramel mixture, spooning circles over the remaining pecans.

4. Meanwhile, microwave the bittersweet chocolate and 2 tablespoons of the shortening in a small microwave-safe bowl at HIGH 30 seconds or until melted. Stir until smooth. Repeat the procedure with the white chocolate and remaining 2 tablespoons shortening. Stir until smooth.

5. Spoon 1 tablespoon chocolate (either bittersweet or white) onto each caramel turtle candy. Sprinkle lightly with coarse sea salt, if desired. Let the candies harden at room temperature (about 1 hour) or in refrigerator before serving.

SALTY CHOCOLATE-PECAN CANDY

Make sure to keep this sweet, salty, crunchy candy in a cool spot to avoid melting.

HANDS-ON TIME 10 MINUTES   TOTAL TIME 1 HOUR 25 MINUTES   MAKES 1¾ POUNDS CANDY

1   cup pecans, coarsely chopped
     Parchment paper
3   (4-ounce) bars bittersweet chocolate baking bars
3   (4-ounce) white chocolate baking bars
1   teaspoon coarse sea salt*

*¾ teaspoon kosher salt may be substituted.

1. Preheat the oven to 350°F. Place the pecans in a single layer on a baking sheet.

2. Bake at 350°F for 8 to 10 minutes or until toasted. Reduce the oven temperature to 225°F.

3. Line a 17- x 12-inch jelly-roll pan with parchment paper. Break each chocolate bar into 8 equal pieces. (You will have 48 pieces total.) Arrange in a checkerboard pattern in the jelly-roll pan, alternating white and dark chocolate. (The pieces will touch.)

4. Bake at 225°F for 5 minutes or just until the chocolate melts. Remove the pan to a wire rack. Swirl the chocolates into a marble pattern using a wooden pick. Sprinkle evenly with the toasted pecans and salt.

5. Chill 1 hour or until firm. Break into pieces. Store in an airtight container in the refrigerator up to 1 month.

TOASTED CHOCOLATE-HAZELNUT FUDGE

Customize this fudge with other nuts or, for picky eaters, leave them out all together.

HANDS-ON TIME 15 MINUTES   TOTAL TIME 1 HOUR 15 MINUTES   MAKES 2 POUNDS CANDY

Cooking spray
Aluminum foil

1   (14-ounce) can sweetened condensed milk

1   (11.5-ounce) package bittersweet chocolate morsels

½   cup chocolate-hazelnut spread

1   cup chopped toasted hazelnuts

1   teaspoon vanilla extract
Pinch of table salt

1. Coat the bottom of an 8-inch square pan with cooking spray. Line the bottom and sides of pan with aluminum foil, allowing 2 to 3 inches to extend over the sides. Coat the foil with cooking spray.

2. Stir together the milk, morsels, and spread in a large heavy saucepan. Cook over medium heat until melted and smooth, about 8 minutes, stirring occasionally. (Mixture will be thick.) Remove from heat; stir in the hazelnuts, vanilla, and salt. Spoon the fudge into the prepared pan. Cover and chill 1 hour or until firm.

3. Lift the fudge from the pan, using the foil sides as handles. Gently remove the foil. Cut the fudge into small squares.

EASY SWIRLED FUDGE

If a thin crust forms on the fudge's surface while microwaving, simply swirl it smooth.

HANDS-ON TIME 20 MINUTES   TOTAL TIME 2 HOURS 25 MINUTES   MAKES ABOUT 1¾ POUNDS CANDY

Parchment paper
½   cup butter
1   (16-ounce) package
    powdered sugar, sifted
½   cup unsweetened cocoa
¼   cup milk
¼   teaspoon table salt
1   tablespoon vanilla extract
1   (4-ounce) white chocolate
    baking bar, chopped
2   tablespoons whipping cream

1. Line the bottom and sides of an 8-inch square pan with parchment paper, allowing 2 to 3 inches to extend over the sides.

2. Microwave the butter in a large microwave-safe bowl at HIGH in 30-second intervals until melted. Gently stir in the powdered sugar and next 3 ingredients. (Mixture will be lumpy.) Microwave 30 seconds; add the vanilla.

3. Beat the mixture at medium-low speed with an electric mixer until well blended and smooth. Pour into the prepared pan, spreading to the edges of the pan.

4. Microwave the white chocolate and whipping cream in a small microwave-safe bowl at HIGH until the white chocolate melts (about 30 seconds to 1 minute), stirring at 30-second intervals. Stir until mixture is smooth. Let stand 1 to 3 minutes or until slightly thickened. Spoon the mixture over the fudge in the pan, swirling with a paring knife. Cover and chill until firm (about 2 hours).

NOTE: We tested in an 1,100-watt and an 1,250-watt microwave oven. Cook times will vary depending on your microwave wattage; be sure to follow the descriptions in the recipe for best results.

BLACK-AND-WHITE PEPPERMINT FUDGE

The marshmallow base in this holiday fudge adds volume and a lighter texture.

HANDS-ON TIME 20 MINUTES   TOTAL TIME 1 HOUR 20 MINUTES   MAKES 2 POUNDS CANDY

Cooking spray

2 cups miniature marshmallows

1¾ cups sugar

¼ cup butter

Pinch of table salt

1 (5-ounce) can evaporated milk

¾ cup bittersweet chocolate morsels

½ teaspoon peppermint extract

¾ cup white chocolate morsels

12 miniature chocolate-covered peppermint patties, chopped

1. Coat an 8-inch square pan with cooking spray.

2. Combine the marshmallows and next 4 ingredients in a large heavy saucepan. Cook over medium, stirring constantly, until the mixture comes to a boil. Boil 6 minutes, stirring constantly. Remove from the heat; pour half of the mixture into a small bowl.

3. Add the bittersweet morsels to half of the marshmallow mixture, stirring until the morsels melt. Stir in the peppermint extract. Spread the mixture into the prepared pan.

4. Stir the white chocolate morsels into the remaining half of the marshmallow mixture, stirring until the morsels melt. Pour the mixture over the chocolate layer in the pan. Sprinkle the chopped peppermint candies over the white chocolate layer. Cover and chill 1 hour or until firm. Cut the fudge into squares.

NOTE: We tested with York Peppermint Patties.

RASPBERRY MARSHMALLOWS

Cut the marshmallows into shapes using lightly greased small cookie cutters.

HANDS-ON TIME 31 MINUTES   TOTAL TIME 12 HOURS 36 MINUTES   MAKES 54 MARSHMALLOWS

Aluminum foil
Cooking spray
- ¾ cup fresh raspberries
- ½ cup plus 2 tablespoons powdered sugar
- 1 cup cold water
- 3 envelopes unflavored gelatin
- 2 cups granulated sugar
- ⅔ cup light corn syrup
- ¼ teaspoon table salt
- 1 teaspoon vanilla extract
- ½ cup cornstarch

1. Line the bottom and sides of a 13- x 9-inch pan with aluminum foil, allowing 2 to 3 inches to extend over the sides; lightly coat the foil with cooking spray.

2. Process the raspberries and 2 tablespoons powdered sugar in a blender or food processor until smooth. Pour the raspberry mixture through a wire-mesh strainer into a bowl, using the back of a spoon to squeeze out the juice. Discard the pulp and seeds.

3. Place ½ cup cold water in the bowl of a heavy-duty electric stand mixer fitted with a whisk attachment. Sprinkle the gelatin over the water; let stand 5 minutes.

4. Combine the granulated sugar, corn syrup, salt, and remaining ½ cup cold water in a medium saucepan. Bring to a boil over medium, stirring occasionally until the sugar dissolves. Cook, without stirring, until a candy thermometer registers 240°F, about 6 minutes. Remove from the heat.

5. With the mixer on low speed, slowly pour the hot syrup in a thin stream over the gelatin mixture. Increase the speed to medium-high, and beat until thick and stiff, about 8 minutes. Beat in the raspberry puree and vanilla. Quickly pour the marshmallow mixture into the prepared pan, smoothing the top with a lightly greased spatula.

6. Combine the remaining ½ cup powdered sugar and cornstarch in a small bowl. Dust the top of the marshmallow mixture in the pan with about ⅓ cup powdered sugar mixture. Let the marshmallows stand, uncovered, 12 hours or overnight.

7. Lift the marshmallows from the pan using foil sides as handles; flip onto a cutting board. Gently remove the foil. Dust the marshmallows with ⅓ cup powdered sugar mixture. Cut into 1½-inch squares using a lightly greased knife. Dust the cut sides of the marshmallows with the remaining powdered sugar mixture.

PEPPERMINT MERINGUES

Make sure your bowls are clean because any trace amounts of fat will wreck the airy batter.

HANDS-ON TIME 25 MINUTES   TOTAL TIME 5 HOURS 10 MINUTES   MAKES 60 MERINGUES

Parchment paper

3   large egg whites, at room temperature

¼   teaspoon cream of tartar

¼   teaspoon peppermint extract

Dash of table salt

½   cup sugar

¼   teaspoon red liquid food coloring

1. Preheat the oven to 175°F. Line 2 large baking sheets with parchment paper.

2. Beat the egg whites and cream of tartar at medium speed with an electric mixer until soft peaks form. Add the peppermint extract and salt, beating until blended. Gradually add the sugar, 2 tablespoons at a time, beating at high speed until stiff glossy peaks form and the sugar dissolves. Spoon half of the meringue into a medium bowl, and add the food coloring. Beat until well blended.

3. In a large decorating bag fitted with a #827 star tip, place spoonfuls of white and red meringue side by side, alternating the colors and working up from the tip of the bag. Do not mix the colors together. Pipe the meringue into 1-inch mounds on the prepared baking sheets.

4. Bake at 175°F for 3 hours or until the meringues are dry to the touch. Turn the oven off; let the meringues stand in the closed oven 1 hour. Finish cooling at room temperature (about 45 minutes). Remove the meringues from the parchment paper. Store in an airtight container at room temperature.

CHOCOLATE-HAZELNUT MERINGUES

For voluminous meringues, pipe the mixture without touching the paper-lined surface.

HANDS-ON TIME 20 MINUTES   TOTAL TIME 3 HOURS 55 MINUTES   MAKES 40 MERINGUES

Parchment paper
4   large egg whites, at room temperature
½   teaspoon cream of tartar
½   cup granulated sugar
½   cup powdered sugar
2   tablespoons unsweetened baking cocoa
½   cup finely chopped toasted hazelnuts

1. Preheat the oven to 225°F. Line baking sheets with parchment paper.

2. Beat the egg whites and cream of tartar at high speed with an electric mixer until foamy. Gradually add 2 tablespoons granulated sugar, 1 tablespoon at a time, beating at medium speed until soft peaks form. Gradually add the remaining 6 tablespoons granulated sugar, powdered sugar, and cocoa, 1 tablespoon at a time, beating at high speed until stiff peaks form and the sugar dissolves (2 to 4 minutes). Fold in the hazelnuts.

3. Spoon the mixture into a decorating bag fitted with a large open star tip. Pipe or dollop the mixture 1 inch apart onto the prepared baking sheets.

4. Bake at 225°F for 1 hour 35 minutes. Turn the oven off; let meringues stand in the closed oven 2 hours. Store tightly covered at room temperature up to 1 week.

NOT YOUR GRANDMA'S DIVINITY

Measure all your ingredients before you start—feather-light divinity requires accuracy.

HANDS-ON TIME 25 MINUTES   TOTAL TIME 12 HOURS 25 MINUTES   MAKES ABOUT 1 POUND CANDY

2 cups sugar
½ cup light corn syrup
⅓ cup water
   Plastic wrap
2 large egg whites
1 teaspoon vanilla extract
   Waxed paper

PECAN-ORANGE DIVINITY

MAKES ABOUT 1 POUND CANDY

Stir in ½ cup toasted chopped pecans and 1 teaspoon grated orange rind after adding the vanilla. Proceed with the recipe as directed.

1. Stir together the sugar, corn syrup, and ⅓ cup water in a 3-quart microwave-safe bowl. Cover with plastic wrap; microwave at HIGH 3 minutes. Uncover and microwave at HIGH 6 to 7½ minutes or until the mixture begins to turn light brown around the edges.

2. Meanwhile, beat the egg whites at high speed with an electric mixer until stiff peaks form (about 4 minutes).

3. Pour the hot sugar mixture in a thin stream over the beaten egg whites, beating at high speed. Add the vanilla, and beat just until the mixture holds its shape (about 3 to 4 minutes). Working quickly, drop the mixture by rounded tablespoonfuls onto waxed paper. Let stand at room temperature until the candies feel firm (at least 12 hours or overnight) before removing from the waxed paper. Store in an airtight container at room temperature.

NOTE: We tested using an 1100-watt microwave oven and a KitchenAid mixer. We recommend using the mixer's wire whisk attachment for beating the egg whites to stiff peaks, and then switching to the paddle attachment while continuing to beat until the candy holds its shape.

METRIC EQUIVALENTS

The recipes that appear in this cookbook use the standard U.S. method for measuring liquid and dry or solid ingredients (teaspoons, tablespoons, and cups). The information in the following charts is provided to help cooks outside the United States successfully use these recipes. All equivalents are approximate.

Metric Equivalents for Different Types of Ingredients

A standard cup measure of a dry or solid ingredient will vary in weight depending on the type of ingredient. A standard cup of liquid is the same volume for any type of liquid. Use the following chart when converting standard cup measures to grams (weight) or milliliters (volume).

Standard Cup	Fine Powder (ex. flour)	Grain (ex. rice)	Granular (ex. sugar)	Liquid Solids (ex. butter)	Liquid (ex. milk)
1	140 g	150 g	190 g	200 g	240 ml
¾	105 g	113 g	143 g	150 g	180 ml
⅔	93 g	100 g	125 g	133 g	160 ml
½	70 g	75 g	95 g	100 g	120 ml
⅓	47 g	50 g	63 g	67 g	80 ml
¼	35 g	38 g	48 g	50 g	60 ml
⅛	18 g	19 g	24 g	25 g	30 ml

Useful Equivalents for Dry Ingredients by Weight

(To convert ounces to grams, multiply the number of ounces by 30.)

1 oz	=	1/16 lb	=	30 g
4 oz	=	¼ lb	=	120 g
8 oz	=	½ lb	=	240 g
12 oz	=	¾ lb	=	360 g
16 oz	=	1 lb	=	480 g

Useful Equivalents for Length

(To convert inches to centimeters, multiply the number of inches by 2.5.)

1 in			=	2.5 cm		
6 in	=	½ ft	=	15 cm		
12 in	=	1 ft	=	30 cm		
36 in	=	3 ft	= 1 yd	90 cm		
40 in			=	100 cm	=	1 m

Useful Equivalents for Liquid Ingredients by Volume

¼ tsp				=	1 ml	
½ tsp				=	2 ml	
1 tsp				=	5 ml	
3 tsp	=	1 Tbsp		=	½ fl oz	= 15 ml
		2 Tbsp	= ⅛ cup	=	1 fl oz	= 30 ml
		4 Tbsp	= ¼ cup	=	2 fl oz	= 60 ml
		5⅓ Tbsp	= ⅓ cup	=	3 fl oz	= 80 ml
		8 Tbsp	= ½ cup	=	4 fl oz	= 120 ml
		10⅔ Tbsp	= ⅔ cup	=	5 fl oz	= 160 ml
		12 Tbsp	= ¾ cup	=	6 fl oz	= 180 ml
		16 Tbsp	= 1 cup	=	8 fl oz	= 240 ml
		1 pt	= 2 cups	=	16 fl oz	= 480 ml
		1 qt	= 4 cups	=	32 fl oz	= 960 ml
					33 fl oz	= 1000 ml = 1 l

Useful Equivalents for Cooking/Oven Temperatures

	Fahrenheit	Celsius	Gas Mark
Freeze water	32° F	0° C	
Room temperature	68° F	20° C	
Boil water	212° F	100° C	
Bake	325° F	160° C	3
	350° F	180° C	4
	375° F	190° C	5
	400° F	200° C	6
	425° F	220° C	7
	450° F	230° C	8
Broil			Grill

INDEX